Praise for *Happily Ever After Divorce*

"Jessica Bram has written the book I wish I'd read twenty years ago, when I embarked on the lonely, scary, and guilt-inducing journey of divorce, in a landscape filled with finger-wagging doomsayers. Without ignoring the sorrow that comes with the death of a marriage—and the complex and occasionally brutal experience of shepherding children through the breakup of a family—Bram offers radical news: the journey can bring not only pain but relief, transformation, and happiness.

"I'd recommend this thoughtful, wise, and tender book to any man or woman going through divorce. Keep it next to the bed, to read and reread during those moments (and they will come) when you ask yourself, 'Will I ever feel okay again? Will my children be damaged forever?' Good news awaits."

—Joyce Maynard, author of
At Home in the World and *To Die For*

"Going from the tidy and coveted 'married-with-kids' scenario to 'divorced-and-winging-it' is a bitter, hellish journey for many. Not so for Ms. Bram, who, after her marriage ends, finds herself slowly resurrecting pieces of her lost self, reconnecting honestly with loved ones, and creating a life in which she feels like herself again. It is a triumphant journey: the transformation of a wife into a woman."

—Dalma Heyn, author of *Marriage Shock:
The Transformation of Women into Wives* and
The Erotic Silence of the American Wife

"Jessica Bram's *Happily Ever After Divorce* is an open, honest, touching, and frequently humorous collection of smart essays about what every woman needs to know . . . what it is like to go through and get through a divorce while keeping yourself not only intact but strong and secure. Ms. Bram shares her journey and along the way we see how this process fills her with awe and appreciation.

"Women reading her essays will feel less alone. They will empathize with Ms. Bram's process and feel inspired and empowered as they witness the roller coaster of emotions that came from her realization that just because a marriage is ending, life not only continues but in many ways, truly begins again. Ms. Bram's candid tone and accessible style invite the reader to want to know more about her as they find out more about themselves in the process.

"By understanding how Ms. Bram approached her divorce, her ex-husband, her children, her employment possibilities, her social life, and her life in general, readers will learn ways to approach their own situations with a fresh eye and confidence. She offers the reader choices about how to live their lives and to consider divorce because it just may be the best option."

—Dale Atkins, Ph.D., psychologist and relationship
expert frequently seen on NBC's *Today Show*,
and author of several books including *Sanity Savers:*
Tips for Women to Lead a Balanced Life

Happily Ever After Divorce

Notes of a Joyful Journey

Jessica Bram

Health Communications, Inc.
Deerfield Beach, Florida

www.hcibooks.com

Library of Congress Cataloging-in-Publication Data

Bram, Jessica.
  Happily ever after divorce : notes of a joyful journey / Jessica Bram.
    p. cm.
    ISBN-13: 978-0-7573-0758-4 (trade paper)
    ISBN-10: 0-7573-0758-2 (trade paper)
  1. Divorce.   2. Self-reliance.   I. Title.
  HQ814.B695 2009
  306.89092—dc22
  [B]   2008049575

Publisher: Health Communications, Inc.
          3201 S.W. 15th Street
          Deerfield Beach, FL 33442-8190

Cover design by Larissa Hise Henoch
Interior design and formatting by Dawn Von Strolley Grove

For my mother,

Risha Granat Shaw—for wisdom,

but mostly, for love

Contents

Acknowledgments

I could fill a second volume with my gratitude for those individuals who made this book possible. Only with the guidance and loving support of certain angels in my life did the dream of this book become reality.

I wish to thank, first and foremost, the dear friends who believed in me as a writer long before I believed in myself: Jane Pollak and Donna Sapolin. This book is the direct result of your faith and encouragement. Thanks also to Lucy Hedrick for envisioning and believing in this book, and contributing so capably to making it real.

My deepest gratitude goes to my teacher and mentor, Suzanne Hoover, Ph.D., who taught me every single thing I know today about writing and teaching, and continues to guide me with her brilliance and wisdom. Suzanne not only contributed to the final shaping of this book, but also fired my own passion to guide other writers as she so lovingly guided me. Not a day goes by when I am not reminded how profoundly fortunate I am to have found Suzanne on my path.

Thank you to the writers in my writing groups who over the years offered their insight and encouragement in shaping the chapters of this book: Karen Davidov and Margaret Pierpont; also Debbie Danowski, Aly Dunne, Lucy Hedrick, Joanne Kabak, and Jane Pollak. While writing itself is a solitary act, there is little I have accomplished alone.

Thank you to my sister Karyn Seroussi, who grew up to be

my dearest friend as well as my role model for the published author and confident woman, who gives others so much more than she receives. I am most grateful to my brothers, Eric Bram and Matthew Bram, who shared those taxi rides and have always stood by me with loyalty and love, no matter what. Loving thanks also to my mother, for her unconditional love, and to Howard Shaw, for being part of our family.

The joyful journey would never have been possible at all without the wisdom and guidance of Graciela Abelin, M.D., and Gilbert Rose, M.D. I know you have found yourself in many pages of this book. Your gifts will continue to reverberate for the rest of my life and those of my sons.

Even when my family was being dismantled and rearranged, certain friends have been my most steadfast family. I will always be grateful to my treasured "sisters," Shirlee Hauser, along with Gillian Anderson, Doreen Birdsell, Raina D'Amico, Betsy Krobot, Jane Pollak, Linda Gramatky Smith, Erika Steffen, and Noreen Sutton, who stood by me "in sickness and in health".

Thank you to Dale Atkins, Ph.D., for your wisdom and generosity, and for being the shining example of what any woman—myself especially—would most hope to become.

Thank you to Gordon Joseloff, for his friendship and support, and for valuable lessons about writing in short paragraphs and AP Style.

I am continually awestruck by how gifted I am to have two brilliant midwives for this book. Thank you to Sharlene Martin of Martin Literary Management, indisputably the "Gold Standard" of literary agents, for her belief in this book and her expert guidance. My immense gratitude also goes to my skillful and supportive editor and now friend, Michele Matrisciani of Health Communications, Inc., for "getting" this book and for bringing it into being. Thank you to my publisher Health Communications, Inc., for sending these and so many other messages of hope out to the world.

A loving thank you to Bob Cooper, whose steadfast support, patience, and love truly gave me my Happily Ever After, as well as the final happy chapter of this book.

I wish also to acknowledge the loving memory of my father, Leonard S. Bram, and my beloved grandmother, Seri Granat.

Finally, my deepest love and gratitude to my sons, David, Robert, and Alex, who gave me my most important and rewarding role in life, and continue to give meaning to every moment.

Introduction: Into the Sunlight

One day, at age forty-one, with three young children, I took a terrifying, guilt-inducing leap. After years of unhappiness, I finally found the courage to get out of my marriage.

It was hard, no question. Hard like childbirth, like building a skyscraper or perhaps demolishing one. As hard as any of the most formidable challenges I had ever faced—every college or graduate school degree, every major disruption, every relocation, every turnaround.

But then, as after childbirth, a glorious new life emerged—but this time, my own. After my divorce I emerged into sunlight, stunned and blinking. Disoriented, yes, and many, many times afraid. But only then did life begin. Only then did I start to piece together, for the first time ever, a life that had fresh air and laughter, challenges and triumphs. A life of outer joys and for the first time, inner peace.

I am here to say that it can be done.

The Light Bulb Problem

Maybe I was imagining it. But damned if every bulb in my house didn't start blowing the week my husband moved out. The problem was so persistent that for a while I even suspected some kind of sabotage on my husband's part. But my friend Eve assured me otherwise. "Bulbs blow out all the time. That's what they do," she said.

Well, of course I knew that bulbs blew out. But my perception after nineteen years of marriage was that soon after they always somehow became replaced. My husband prided himself on his skills in home repair, and I had long been secure in the knowledge that just say the word, and rooms that were temporarily dark would soon once again be light. Just as dripping faucets would eventually stop leaking and overflowing roof gutters made clear. There never seemed to be any question that these tasks, which my husband performed with cheerful vigor, were his preordained responsibility, separate and mysterious.

Certainly changing a light bulb—or any home maintenance task, for that matter—is hardly a question of gender. I know a multitude of men without the slightest interest in home repair. "You have to understand," replied the former owner of our house, when we questioned him about the wiring, "I called an electrician when a light bulb burned out." And my mother, who raised three children alone back in the fifties when everyone else, it seemed, had a father mowing the lawn and replacing storm windows, handled a lot more than light bulbs. I remember my mother in her long swishy dress, dreamily moving back and forth to the sound of Mantovani strings on the hi-fi, measuring, marking pencil spots on the wall, wielding a heavy electric drill to mount bookshelves. And today I know more than a few women like my younger sister, more adept at carpentry, electric wiring, and telephone installation than many nonprofessionals, my former husband included.

But my sister lived seven hours away and wasn't there to advise me when all my bulbs began going dark. My house required a staggering variety of bulbs. Beside conventional bulbs in all wattages, my light fixtures called for broad-faced recessed floods, spots, and reflectors, both direct and indirect; skinny undercounter fluorescents in varying lengths; round vanity bulbs, frosted and clear; bulbs that hid above semiopaque ceiling panels; microwave bulbs and refrigerator bulbs and even night-light bulbs the size of a thumb. (It never occurred to me one could actually replace a night-light bulb—night-lights always just seemed to *be* there, eternal and trust-worthy.) Most daunting of all were two large ornamental wrought iron and glass lanterns residing on either side of the front door, each containing within its narrow interior a cluster of small flame-shaped bulbs. When these giant fixtures began to dim, I would stand beneath them, night after night, contemplating how one could possibly squeeze one's hand into slim crevices at the bottom to replace the tiny glass flames.

The gradual darkening of my home went on for weeks, during which time I left the dead bulbs alone. I suppose I was imagining, against all reason, that my husband would simply reappear in jeans one Saturday morning with his aluminum ladder to fix the problem as he always had. I was tempted to call him and say, "Look, everything else aside, could you please come and change the bulbs?" But of course this was impossible.

Why, I wondered, was the sight of these dark bulbs so full of ill portent? Whenever I received no response to an overhead switch or found a dark shadow across my kitchen counter where there should have been a strong fluorescent beam, I shuddered. I had always hated dim light in general, but now more than ever these dead bulbs seemed to remind me of desolate places like musty hotel rooms and nighttime bus stations.

Eventually each dark corner or black closet interior in my house would confront me like a reproach: what are you going to do about this? Finally one late evening, as I carried my towel-wrapped two-year-old son from the bath, I reached for the switch in his room and encountered that awful pop and brief, loud spark, followed by darkness.

Standing in the dark with my child in my arms, I faced the dismal truth: No one is going to fix this but you. He's not around to do this any more.

As luck would have it, there was a spare bulb behind the vacuum cleaner bags in the broom closet. And of course, it did not take long to figure out that replacing the rest of the bulbs in the house was no big deal. I soon learned that there was always someone at the hardware or lighting store who could identify and procure a required bulb. Back home, using a step stool or more often a kitchen chair, I'd screw the new one in. Problem solved: light where there was dark. I realized that in a house with leaking pipes and an aging septic system, the satisfaction derived from replacing a bulb was instantaneous. An easy high.

But what most came to mind as I brought my house back to light was the memory of my mother with her electric drill. I knew back then that this was not what most mothers did. I never saw any of my friends' mothers, or Donna Reed or Lucy Ricardo for that matter, sinking anchors into sheetrock for bookshelves. But watching my mother, after a long afternoon of drilling, slip each metal bracket into its slot with a satisfied expression, hearing those definite metallic clicks as she locked each one into place, I was proud. Maybe we didn't have a father in the house to protect us from ceiling leaks or from harm. But if my mother could build a wall of shelves, I knew she could do anything. We would be all right.

And finally, as I reached high from a chair in my son's room and gave the smooth new bulb in my hand that final twist that brings it back to life, instantly turning it from cold to warm, from gray to white, I realized it comes down to this: Each dark spot extinguished quenches a worry, each dark room illuminated quells a doubt. If I alone could bring this house back to light, perhaps I, too, could banish my sons' middle-of-the-night fears as well as their father once did when he carried them back to their beds with strong arms. Perhaps I would banish my own.

And when, for the rest of that long winter, I drove to my front door late at night to see every flame bulb in our lanterns, every last one of them, glowing brightly—when late at night, I would flip the switch in my dark kitchen to be greeted by an unwavering line of undercabinet light—I knew that in this house, in this home, all was well.

The Journey

On April 1, 1998, I sat in my car on Bay Street staring unbelieving at a piece of paper in my hands. It was the deed to a house, and the title was in my name—and my name only. No joint ownership, no second position after a husband's name—just mine. It was thrilling. And it was terrifying.

It felt like the worst day of my life. Or maybe it was the best day. I couldn't be sure.

I had just emerged from a lawyer's office where for two hours I had been signing documents and writing checks. Only in the car, after every document was signed, mortgage committed to, and title passed, did the enormity of what I had just done come over me.

I had just bought a new house where my sons and I would go to live after my divorce. The house—a small house in need of repair, in a strange new neighborhood and new town where we knew no one—was ours. Mine.

What had I been thinking? Too late to go back! The paper in my hands shook.

Long-held-back tears began to drip onto the new deed as I thought of how much had gone into this moment—how much work and struggle; how many misgivings and self-doubts. How many arguments, and dreaded appointments, and phone conversations, and court meetings. The endless legal documents faxed to my lawyer and back again. I thought of how many times I had felt absolutely unfit to take one more step forward, how many nights I had cried inside. *No! I can't do this! Why did I think I could do this?*

But I had done it. Here was proof in black and white, with a freshly embossed, notarized seal. My diploma, in a way. I had pushed on and gotten through it all and here I was, with my name typed at the top of the title to a certain property known as lot thirty-two on Volume 6283 of my new town's land records.

The task before me was daunting. I would have to pack up a large house and move us. I would have to get three sons enrolled and settled in a new school, one in first grade, and two in middle school. My sons, especially the thirteen-year-old, were unhappy about moving to a town where they would have to make new friends. I would have to find a new pediatrician, pharmacy, gym, orthodontist. I had a new mortgage but with no job—my only income source was a *pendente lite* temporary child support order—I was not clear about how I would be able to pay my monthly payments.

What I did not know at that moment, shaking in my car, was that despite how miserable and scared I felt at that moment, despite the "What have I done?" sense of alarm, this was truly the best day of my life. Because it was the day I began my new life. I didn't yet know that this new life ahead of me in unknown terrain wouldn't turn out to be the disaster I had feared through all those years of a troubled marriage and all those dark nights of a painful divorce. It would not take long to discover that this new life—for the first time, a life of my own creation—would be a thousandfold better than any I ever had before.

We had been married nineteen years, and the marriage had been on shaky ground from the start. I had gotten married at the impossibly young age of twenty-two, only two years out of college, and with no idea where I was to go or how I was to earn a living. The country was in a recession, and meaningful jobs for recent college graduates were nonexistent. Not that I had the slightest idea what kind of job I wanted. I quickly abandoned the idea of law school, a halfhearted goal I had given lip service to all through college only to mollify my father.

Instead, I paid a visit that fall, about the same time I was to have started law school, to a kindly young graduate student—I will refer to him as Bill—whom I had dated for a few weeks after graduation. Bill was a good, companionable friend, although hardly a soul mate. A two-week visit turned into two years of living together. Then one day I found myself in a white Mexican cotton wedding dress, standing alongside my father just outside the door of the St. Moritz Terrace Room, listening to the strains of the Pachelbel's Canon from the next room.

I was racked with indecision. Was I meant to be with

this man? Was I about to make a mistake? And wasn't the idea of a perfect soul mate some kind of romantic fiction, anyway? If I didn't marry him, then what would I do? I drew a blank.

Oh, hell, I thought. *If it doesn't work out, I can always get a divorce.* And proceeded down the aisle.

I was to remember those words many times over the next nineteen years as we visited a variety of marriage counselors and spent many silent dinners in restaurants and many long nights engaged in strained conversations. We seemed to need constant mediation for every issue— everything from where we would live—he hated the city, I couldn't imagine living anywhere else—to how high to turn the burner under a frying pan. We disappointed each other in myriad ways. We put off having children for almost nine years. The excuse I gave, to the world and to myself, was that I was committed to developing a career of my own. But deep inside I knew that the marriage could not last, and I could not bear the thought of ever subjecting children to divorce.

Eventually, the years of recriminations and disappointments chipped away at love, until little, if any, remained. I took comfort in friendships and comfortable companionship with Bill. There was the security of routine. We began to gain a financially solid ground and spent money on home renovations and interesting travel. Days and weekends were filled with activities that could distract me from the quiet, regretful ache of the absence of passion.

Then came my thirties, and with the clock ticking, I figured, *If I haven't left him yet, I guess I never will.* I became pregnant quickly and easily. Bill and I became submerged in the joys of parenthood, along with the round-the-clock challenge of caring for first one, then two, then three babies over the next twelve years. Bill turned out to be a great father. Most important, there was now love in our lives—a huge groundswell of love for our sons. Our mutual adoration of those little boys, with their wet, combed hair and clean pajamas after bath time, blocked out any thought of what was missing in the marriage. Life felt, in a way, ordered and complete.

Looking back now, I envision us standing alongside each other all those years, not touching but facing in the same direction. Focusing first on the challenges of parenthood, and then on growing his real estate business, which I joined when my first son was born. We made money and were able to afford household help, which alleviated the stress of caring for our children while running a business. We moved into a bigger house in the country. We were united, if not in marital bliss, then a satisfying commonality of purpose in the world. Happily married or not, I vowed—swore!—to avoid divorce at all costs. I would never take my sons away from their father. I would do whatever was necessary to preserve for our children the good life we had built for them.

"Man makes plans, and God laughs" according to a Yiddish expression. My husband did love our sons, fully and completely. Perhaps Bill thought, as I myself came to believe, that love for children could substitute for the huge, gaping hole created by the lack of adult love and grown-up passion. For a number of years, it did.

When he wasn't immersed in newspapers, Bill spent

long weekend hours with our boys, teaching them to garden with him or ride bikes. He supervised lengthy, activity-filled bath times and spent evenings reading to each in turn before tucking them into bed at night. Often after Bill came back to his newspapers, I would go upstairs for my turn to kiss them good night but found the boys already asleep.

Slowly I began to feel that I lived alongside a separate, loving family, consisting of a gentle father and his three sons. A family that excluded me. Except for getting dinner on the table where my sons and their father could engage in private jokes and discussions of school, sports, and world events, I felt extraneous. While cozy bedtime stories were told upstairs, I would stand in my clean kitchen, filling backpacks with the next day's snacks and permission slips, loneliness eating away at me.

Eventually the ache of being without love began to throb inside me like a wound that not only did not heal, but deepened. I began, longingly, to notice other men.

When our marriage finally did come apart, it was nothing short of a mess. Nineteen years later, for the first time, I came to fully understand the folly of my "Oh, hell, if it doesn't work out, I can always get a divorce" idea. Dividing assets, which included the big house and the real estate business, was highly complicated and very soon became contentious. Despite our guilty, teary assurances to our children that both parents loved them, that they would never lose either of us, we were equally depressed about what damage might be done to our little boys. Financial realities of dividing one home into two began to sink in. And at the same time, we were facing the end of the dream life—with a nineteen-year marriage and near-perfect home—we had tried so hard to create.

Not long after we announced our divorce, the ominous chorus of naysaying began. Shortly after Bill moved out, we consulted a child psychologist for guidance on how to protect our children from the fallout. He was like a physician announcing the cancer had spread beyond hope. "It's going to be hell," he intoned with great solemnity. A neighbor warned, "Be careful—the kids who get into trouble are usually the ones from divorced homes." More than a few people cited statistics helpfully informing me what percentage—it ranged from 50 to 75 percent—of divorced women end up below the poverty line.

If life was unhappy before, now it was nothing short of miserable. Suddenly I had a new full-time job furnishing my lawyer with financial records and other documents. From nights of panicked eating, I began gaining serious weight. Not that it mattered how I looked, since single friends were quick to warn me about dating. "Wait till you see what's out there. The good ones are all married, and the rest of them all want younger women." A few timid peeks at online dating services made me realize that a single woman with three young children need not even bother to pay the membership fee. "We have not found a suitable match for you that meets our excruciating standards" (or something to that effect) announced the message on eHarmony, night after night until my fifty dollar, one-month trial membership expired, with not a single match produced.

The divorce stretched out two years, then three, then four. Not much more needs to be written about it other than it was as miserable as divorces inevitably are. Many times I wanted to back out of it, apologize, ask him to move back home, say "Let's make all this disappear." Once or twice I even did. Occasionally we would make a feeble attempt at a reconciliatory drink or dinner, only to end up bitterly rehashing old conflicts. At times I was sure that by going ahead with the divorce I had made a terrible mistake, destroyed my life and my children's lives, and just awoken, as if from a dream, and wondered, *What have I done?*

There is a moment in labor, when the baby is still a long time from coming, but the contractions are so punishing and so excruciatingly cruel that you want to scream, "That's it! I'm done! I'm out of here!" But there is absolutely no getting out of here, no backing out. Nowhere to go but forward into even crueler and more punishing waves of pain. That's what my divorce felt like at times. And there were times, too, when I thought of a strange children's book I would read my boys when they were little called *We're Going on a Bear Hunt*. It was about a family that would encounter swampy fields, rushing ponds, muddy bogs, and scary caves, on their adventure looking for a bear. "We can't go over it. We can't go under it. Oh no! We've got to go through it," they would sing-song at each scary obstacle. So I would remind myself at each weak, faltering, terrified, unsteady moment in my divorce, as I headed into an uncertain and what seemed at times to be a disastrous future, *I can't go over it, I can't go under it, I've got to go through it.*

Despite the naysayers, there were a few voices that assured me I would get through it. While I was timidly exercising that muscle that would slowly grow into a new sense of self, I called on my family and my true friends. When late at night I ran out of red wine or Ben & Jerry's New York Super Fudge Chunk, and the tears would come, I'd call my sister in upstate New York, or my friend Donna a few streets away, or my mother in Florida. "I am no match for all this," I would cry. "My husband wants to destroy me, this will destroy me. I will never get through this."

"Yes, Jessica, you will get through this," they said.

And I did get through it. I moved on. And then my good life—great and joyful life—began.

I offer you highlights of my rocky, joyful journey. The message is this: You can't go over it. You can't go under it. You've got to go through it. And you *will* get through it. And wait—just wait!—to see what riches you will find.

Banish the Naysayers

As if I didn't feel bad enough about my divorce, the whole world seemed to be conspiring to make me feel worse. Like the engraved acrylic sign on the reception desk of the pediatric ophthalmologist (yes, someone had actually taken the trouble to have it permanently imprinted):

Notice to Divorced Parents: Payment is the responsibility of the parent accompanying the patient and must be paid in full prior to service.

Until that moment, all I had been thinking of was the note sent home by David's first-grade teacher saying that he seemed to have some trouble reading the board. Despite some of Bill's and my ugly arguments about money during our divorce, I knew that the last thing either of us would ever object to paying for was anything related to the children's health. But this sign seemed to brand me as a criminal the moment I walked in the door.

My humiliation turned to outrage. Talk about kicking people when they're down.

I confronted the receptionist: "How can you single out divorced patients like that?" I asked. She answered curtly. "We've had too many instances of our bills going unpaid because there's a dispute over which divorced parent is supposed to pay for the appointment. We just can't get into that."

Then there was the marriage counselor Bill and I consulted in the last, unhappy days of our marriage. One need not have been a professional to see that the marriage was past the point of no return. But for our children's sake, we were determined to leave no stone unturned in a desperate attempt to avoid the inevitable. For well over an hour, we went at each other tooth and nail. Every resentment, lie, grievance, and accusation surfaced. The bitterness and hostility flowed freely. For most of this, the therapist stayed silent.

Finally, she spoke up.

"I must make you both aware that a recent study by Dr. Judith Wallerstein has shown that divorce is far more damaging to children than had been previously thought. In fact, it's the single most traumatic event that can happen in a child's life. Not just that, but also that the negative effects of divorce are long lasting and profound. . . ." Her words became an unintelligible blur, punctuated by phrases like *struggle at school, drug and alcohol abuse, inability to form attachments in later years, and damage lasting long into adulthood.* For the next ten minutes the therapist went on, citing statistics and more of the famous Dr. Wallerstein's damning conclusions.

Silent, we stared at her. In our session with her, the subject of our children had never come up. Why didn't she just hand us knives so we could slit our wrists right then?

It was hard, in my emotionally worn-out state, not to allow all these naysayers to beat me down even further than I already was. Along with the child psychiatrist who had assured us it was "going to be hell," there were plenty of them. A neighbor responded to the news of our divorce with a distressed, "Oh, dear—and we thought you were such a nice family!" then warned in a whisper how likely it was for children from "broken" homes to have problems with alcohol and drugs. And Dr. Wallerstein's chilling references to "a society that allows 'divorce on demand'" were a clear battle cry for tighter legal restrictions on divorce. Which would mean that miserable couples like us should just shut up and get used to being miserable.

The world suddenly seemed to see us either as criminals, or carriers of a communicable disease that might infect the neighborhood. It was as though we had violated some fundamental human contract. The message was clear: You are guilty. You must be punished.

As though I wasn't spending enough time fearing poverty, eating my way through loneliness, or recriminating myself for ruining my children's lives, this was the last thing I needed to hear. Even on the good days—days that I felt mostly relief at being free of the strife of my marriage, there would inevitably come some sorrowful "I'm so sorry!" to once more deepen my sense of guilt.

But there was a day I received an entirely different

reaction. One spring morning, just before we were to put our marital home on the market, I spotted our gardener through the window. He was working at his usual leisurely pace among the flower beds in front of the house. Small and somewhat stooped, with swarthy skin weathered from a lifetime working outdoors, Anthony had taken care of the property for over two decades, long before we bought it. Many families had come and gone over the years. Now I had to let him know the house, which we had owned for less than two years, would be once more sold. Dreading having to announce our impending divorce one more time yet again, I stepped outside to speak to him.

Hearing the news, Anthony cocked his head slightly, his expression remaining pleasant. Then he shrugged. "It happens," he said.

There seemed nothing more to say. Anthony bent down and continued what he was doing. In the silence, I looked down and noticed, for the first time, the bed of fat, brilliant blossoms that Anthony had been working on. Some were a vibrant candy-heart pink; others, creamy white, were delicately streaked with scarlet. Until I had come out to stand this close to them, I hadn't noticed how breathtakingly beautiful they were, plump, and at the same time, each petal as delicate as porcelain.

"These are gorgeous, Anthony. What are they called?"

"Peonies," he said, then bent down to pick off a head that was already beginning to fade. "You don't know peonies? They're perennials. Come up every year. Each year there's more, better each time. Here, smell," he said, handing me the blossom.

I breathed in the sweetness, which had the delicate scent of fresh cream mixed with my grandmother's White Shoulders Dusting Powder. For the moment, my divorce seemed something very far away.

In calmer and more rational times, I look back on all the negative comments made about my divorce in those early months following our announcement. The comments didn't make sense. This wasn't like the old days, when my mother had been ashamed to use the word *divorce*. With divorce now so prevalent, wouldn't you think it would have become more accepted? Why this persistent stigma?

I suppose the reaction has mostly to do with fear. If it could happen to us ("Such a nice family!"), it could happen to anyone, right? Just think, all those women surrounding me who had given up careers to raise children—and there were plenty of them in our well-to-do town—could at a moment's notice be forced to fire their housekeepers, put their children in day care, and get jobs selling real estate.

Or is it that society fears bearing the consequences of our potentially divorce-traumatized alcohol and drug-dependent offspring? Perhaps even the ophthalmologist feared having his bills unpaid.

But here's a radical thought—what if someone had told me that I might *not* end up poor after my divorce, that my sons would thrive, and my life would become a thousandfold better than it had ever been before? That I would grow in ways I could never imagine? That I would discover the strength and talents to craft a new life of my own creation? That in moving forward in this divorce, I was doing the right thing? That I was doing what would turn out to be the best for all of us, Bill and the children included?

All of that, and more, is what did come to pass. Even the ophthalmologist got paid—along with a letter directing him to promptly transfer my son's chart to a new doctor.

My good friend Marcella, a bright, funny, creative woman, recently told me she had decided to get a divorce. Her marriage had always been a puzzling partnership to me. Her husband, a pleasant enough man with not a fraction of Marcella's energy or intellect, had not worked for years and was content to let Marcella support him and their daughter. I could hardly imagine any erotic energy generated by this affable deadbeat. Hearing Marcella's news, I had no doubt that this announcement was long overdue—and that life could finally begin for this remarkable woman.

Only one word came to mind. "Congratulations," I blurted out.

Tears sprang to Marcella's eyes. "You're the only one who said that," she said. "All everyone ever says is 'I'm sorry.' And here I feel like I'm finally doing something I've been wishing for years to find the courage to do."

"Listen," I told Marcella. "It happens."

Yes, it happens. And that's when the miracles begin.

No Messages

When one goes from married to no longer married, life changes in hundreds of small and surprising ways. Despite the serious and profound forces that propelled me into divorce—lack of love, betrayal, pain—it was, in fact, how different the myriad unimportant, daily moments were that truly drove home for me what a divorced life would be. My children's school directories now listed their parents' names on two separate lines. My cookbooks with their food-stained pages abruptly went into exile when I began cooking for just myself and the children. As the lone adult in the household I was always, *always* the one to do the driving, no matter the time of day or night, no matter how sleepy or back-sore I became in the driver's seat, heading for a summer beach rental or a family reunion in another state.

But no moment drove home my newly alone state as

deeply as a single moment on a hot, sunny day on the New Jersey Turnpike.

The first year of our separation my children were to be with Bill for the long Memorial Day weekend. In the three free days I would have to myself—the first since having children—I decided to attend a writer's conference at Goucher College in Maryland. In my children's early years I had yearned to take an occasional break from motherhood and go off somewhere to be a writer with a notebook or a book of poetry. I craved any opportunity to become once again, even temporarily, that dreaming, thinking human being I used to be, rather than the toddler-bound, housekeeping cook and bill payer I felt I had become.

Divorce presented the unexpected bonus that this fantasy would be made real. With my children in Bill's custodial care, I would have no responsibilities, none whatsoever, other than to drive to Maryland to begin my transformation into the writer I had all but given up hope of becoming.

I set out early Friday morning, but not early enough to miss the holiday traffic. It was unusually warm for a Memorial Day weekend, and the sun turned hot as it glinted off an increasingly congested stream of autos along the Sprain Brook Parkway to the Henry Hudson Parkway, eventually bumper-to-bumper over the George Washington Bridge. Heading west on Route 80 in New Jersey, past industrial plants and smokestacks, reminding myself to pay close attention, I maneuvered the complicated on-ramps that would lead to the Turnpike rather than the Palisades Interstate Parkway—an easy error, I remembered, that Bill had once made.

In all our years of marriage, Bill had been the primary driver by some unspoken mutual agreement. With no great affection for driving, I was content to stare dreamily out the window or change radio stations or doze while he capably got us where we needed to go. But I was the driver now.

I can do this, I reminded myself, keeping to the center lane as I crossed the George Washington Bridge. *See, there's the sign for the turnpike. Watch carefully where it splits. Stay clear of the trucks and out of the left lane, except to pass. Watch for entering cars. Yes, of course I can do this. I will be fine.*

Although the traffic picked up in New Jersey, I made decent time. Entering Delaware, a sign announced a highway rest stop two miles ahead. Great, perfect. It was too early for lunch, but I could use a stop, a soda maybe. Definitely time for a rest stop. Pleased, I noted that I had made good time. I would reach Maryland by early afternoon, well before registration. There might even be time to see the campus and the town.

It took a few turns to find a spot in the parking lot, already crowded with early summer travelers. The sun beat down on my shoulders and on the metallic sea of autos laden with bike racks and packed with coolers and summer gear. My car had just one overnight bag in the trunk. Several CDs and a map in the front seat, nothing more.

Pay phones lined both sides of the building entrance, thick with a busy stream of incoming rest-stoppers. Yes, a pay phone! I could call to say that I had gotten over the bridge without mishap, had arrived in Delaware safely, and would make it to the conference in plenty of time.

But then I stopped short, facing a phone. Call whom? There was *no one to call.* No one—no family member, no husband, no parent or child—was waiting to hear that I had made it to Delaware safely. No one missed me. I was heading for a weekend with strangers, and not one soul even knew where I was. For the first time in over nineteen years, there was no reason to call the man who had been my husband to tell him where I was. We were no longer married; he wouldn't care.

At that moment the full enormity of how my life *had* changed, how my life *would* change, fully hit me.

I bought a bottle of spring water and headed back to my car, feeling eerie and unreal. The air had gotten so thick and hot, the sun so relentless, that I could barely breathe. I clutched the steering wheel with both hands, put my head down, and felt the throbbing pulse of my own circulation.

There's no one to call. No one to tell. No one knows where I am going or where I am.

After a few long moments in the hot car, my heart began to slow. *Breathe,* I told myself, *breathe. I can do this.*

I had never felt so lost or so alone.

But then I did start to breathe, long, slow, clear breaths. I took a drink of my bottled water. I turned on the engine, and in a few moments cool air began to blow from the vents. I put the car in gear and found my way to the highway. South on the New Jersey Turnpike, watch for the Delaware turnoff, and then it would be a straight run to Maryland. I knew where I was going. And what was the "there" I was heading toward? Well, I thought with a long exhale, I would find out, wouldn't I?

There have been many, many of those moments since then, although none hitting me with quite the intensity of that afternoon on the New Jersey Turnpike. Gradually they hit me with less force, as I became more accustomed to setting out on trips and handling life's daily emergencies. I wish I could say those moments have disappeared forever. But they have not. Little reminders still occasionally catch me unaware. Evenings when my sons are with their father, and I look up from my desk to see that the dinner hour has long passed. Stepping off the train from the city at day's end, weaving through the cars with spouses waiting and engines idling, to find my car at the far end of the dark commuter lot, stone-cold, exactly where I left it. Dialing into voicemail and the prerecorded answer comes back with firm and calm certainty: *no messages.* The words I hear are: *no one is looking for you, no one misses you today, no one wants you.*

But there is another side to those moments, too. I pass through those sometimes disorienting, sometimes frightening stopping points, and when I come out on the other side there is unexpected daylight, and an exhilarating realization that yes, I can do this! Yes, I can find my way back to the highway. Yes, I will get to Maryland, and pick up my keys, and find my room, and spend a fascinating, absorbing weekend with other hopeful writers with unfamiliar faces and brand-new stories, with whom, by the end of the three days, I will exchange pieces of writing and telephone numbers. Yes, I know exactly where I left my car this morning, and yes, here are my keys in my hand, and yes, yes, I can do this!

And sometimes, even—when I've reached the end of a

long highway that traverses an entire state or changed planes in a complicated airport or even just successfully made my case in the tax assessor's office in my own town hall, all by myself, no husband, no friend, just me myself—then sometimes, in moments like that, my heart almost bursts with pride and the powerful recognition that yes, I can do this. I am alone, and yes, by God, I can do this just fine.

Good-Bye Loneliness

The smell of ammonia and vinyl met me as I entered Room 104 of the Sea Shell Motel on the New Jersey shore. The seashell motif was everywhere, from the scallop-bedecked curtains of the shaded window facing the parking lot, to the cockleshells scattered across the translucent blue plastic shower curtain. Conches and clam shells on a background of tan and aquamarine covered the walls. The room was little and airless, and the word *tacky* jumped into my head. I took a deep breath, setting down my one bag. "I'll be all right, I'm all right," I told myself.

It was the first July Fourth weekend that my sons would be with their father. Although four months had passed since we had separated, Bill and I were still mired in divorce proceedings, which by now had gone from well-intentioned to acrimonious. My days were stressed and anxious, filled with expensive phone conferences with my divorce lawyer and lots of worry about the future.

On this Friday morning, without thinking about it for very long, I made an impulsive decision to make the three-hour drive to Long Beach Island on the coast of New Jersey. Although I hadn't been there in years, there was a reason I chose this place. As a child I had spent many summer weekends here with my father and step-mother, who each year rented a tiny second-floor apartment on a quiet sandy street just yards from the beach. I suppose I was hoping to go back to a place and time when life presented, for a summer weekend at least, challenges no more daunting than keeping from tracking sand into the house or where to go for a fried clam dinner. Or perhaps I was seeking out a place where, in my memory, I had felt safe. Although most hotels were full during the high season of summer, there was a room available at the Sea Shell Motel in Beach Haven.

It would be my first vacation, since college, without Bill. At the Goucher College Writers' Conference I had been in the company of other writers, and busy attending lectures and workshops. This time I would be completely alone. I told no one where I was going, not even my lawyer. In those pre–cell phone days, no one would be able to reach me. This was what I wanted. Exhausted from packing up a house and facing a move and the strife of divorce negotiations, I simply wanted time alone. Time to nap, to think, to take my spiral notepad to the beach and make sense of the tangle of my emotions by setting them on paper. But I was apprehensive, too. Would I be lonely? Would I become depressed eating alone in restaurants, occupying one single bed in a motel room, after all these years of being part of a family? I was working so hard every day to keep depression from pulling me under. Would this be an awful mistake?

All I knew was that I needed to get away.

The nondescript Sea Shell Motel had not been hard to find on the main road that ran from the southern tip of Long Beach Island to Barnegat Lighthouse. The L-shaped, pink concrete, single-story building straddled a parking lot. A long row of numbered turquoise doors directly faced each guest's parking spot.

I dropped my bag on the bed and began to unpack. The air conditioner buzzed quietly over the muffled whoosh of cars on the main road outside the motel. I decided to unpack my overnight bag and try to make myself at home, so to speak, in this little vinyl-smelling refuge.

And then something happened. As I emptied my toiletries and began arranging them on the small shelf under the medicine chest, something new and different came over me—a feeling so unfamiliar it was almost shocking. There was, for this moment, for the first time in years—years in which I had shared hotel bathrooms with a man—no tension. No battle. No one to object to how much room on the shelf I was taking up with my moisturizer and suntan lotion, shampoo, and makeup remover. No sidelong glance at my bulging makeup case with raised eyebrows; no sarcastic comment about how many weeks, exactly, I had packed for. This room and this windowless bathroom were all mine and mine alone. I could take up as much room as I liked.

A sense of gladness washed over me in great, soft waves. I could feel my body in one long exhale, as if to say, *I'm safe. The war is over.*

I didn't know then, but that was only the first of many such blessed moments, when I realized, with profound relief, that the space I took up—whether a bathroom sink, room, beach, or restaurant table—was mine alone. I easily fell asleep that night—as I still do—with half of the big bed piled with my book and newspapers—those same newspapers whose crinkling had never failed to annoy my husband—a section spread open on my chest.

Claiming my own space was just the beginning. After all my years of straining my way through a troubled marriage, I now had my very life to myself. Suddenly, my days and nights were free of criticism. Free of sarcasm and innuendo. Free of conflict and complaint. In place of all that conflict, there was silence—not an empty silence, but something rich and luxurious. A sweet, nurturing silence enveloped me like a soft challis scarf around my shoulders.

That first weekend alone on Long Beach Island I was a bit like Helen Keller running from one newly discovered delight to the next. A walk to the beach at my own pace, without skipping to keep up with someone else's impatient stride. Taking all the time I wanted to cruise through beach shops, even if it meant wasting perfectly good beach time, looking at stupid things like lamps made from seashells or lobster shot glasses. Though I was surrounded by couples and two-parent families, even dinners alone in the seaside restaurants didn't faze me. I indulged in as much pointless chitchat with waitresses as I cared to or made my innumerable requests for a better table or dressing on the side or a cleaner water glass without being criticized for being so demanding.

On Saturday evening it was still light out as I walked back to the Sea Shell after dinner at a restaurant with big windows facing quiet Manahawkin Bay. It had been a wonderful meal: clam chowder with two packets of oyster crackers, fried scallops, a glass of cold white wine. I had chatted about careers with the waitress, a cute young college student with a ponytail, who was working to save money for her junior year at Rutgers. A warm glow made up of the salty sea air and evening silence surrounded me all the way home.

Then, with a surprise, a new realization came to me: *I'm not lonely. I thought I would be lonely, but I'm not.* I let out a deep exhale and, with it, seemed to let go of all the unhappiness of those years of my marriage, along with the worry and the conflict over whether I should leave it. I could let go, finally, of the certainty that were I to leave my marriage, I would drown in loneliness. Well, here was my answer. I wasn't lonely, not in the slightest. Not nearly as lonely as I had been in a marriage that wasn't working, where silence had felt like daggers.

But even more, I was not lonely for this reason: I was in good company. The company of my new self, becoming more complete by the minute. It occurred to me, too, that in all those years of my marriage and bearing and raising children, something else had happened that I had not noticed. I had grown up.

In the years that followed the end of my marriage, but especially in those early months after my separation, I was often delightfully astounded by how seldom I was lonely. There was always that tough moment when the boys climbed into their father's car on a Friday evening. But then before I knew it the weekend would fly by, filled with errands and friends and all the wonderful meaningless weekend running-around that I never seemed to have time for when the children were home. I spent luxurious Sunday mornings with the newspaper all to myself, endless coffee—the flavored French vanilla kind that I and no one else liked—and Schubert's Trout Quintet, reveling in peacefulness and ease. Before I knew it Sunday evening would come and the children would be back dropping shoes on the floor, needing dinner and backpacks organized for Monday morning. I would hug their dirty bodies happily before sending them upstairs to their baths.

In the years in which I have rebuilt my life, as both a single woman and a single mother, the moment I often find myself enjoying most is the one in which I enter my bathroom and come upon the creams and the perfumes on the vanity, the stack of eye shadows in far more colors than I'll ever need, and the bouquet of makeup brushes in a floral demitasse cup. Mine and mine alone. They take up just about every inch of space on my small shelf. And there right alongside them, always, is a small seashell.

Coffee with the Enemy

Despite my daily self-admonitions to stay positive, I will admit that the process of legally ending my marriage and dividing our assets was dreary, tedious, and difficult. But without question, the worst of it—the most frightening and tension-producing—the part that hit me most intensely in the gut—was when the issue of the children's custody came up.

"Parental access and custody are very charged issues," my lawyer had warned. Little did I realize at the outset of the discussions not only how charged but hair-trigger explosive these issues could truly be. The heat and energy generated on both sides by custody issues seemed to come from some organic place, fueled by their own internal, combustible power. The same place, no doubt, from which comes that overpowering parental urge to protect our young, even if it means laying down our lives. The way I felt about my children—the way my husband felt about his children . . . there would be little room for rationality here.

Sure enough, it took almost no time at all for our discussions, spearheaded by our lawyers, to turn ugly. As opening gambits, each of our lawyers nudged us toward the most incendiary path possible. For strategic negotiating purposes I was told to demand full custody, even though the last thing I wanted to do was distance my sons from their father. But by asking for full custody and settling for joint, my lawyer explained, we could get something in exchange. It began to feel uncomfortably like a chess game, with my children the pawns who would eventually be knocked off the board.

But it wasn't until a certain phrase was used—Bill's lawyer's opening gambit, no doubt—that I knew that things had gone beyond ugly and were about to spiral out of control. To obtain maximum custodial access to our sons, my husband, it was reported to me via the lawyers, was calling me an "unfit mother."

When my lawyer repeated those words to me, I was sickened to the bottom of my soul. I knew one thing with dead certainty. I knew that Bill, whose sons never missed a meal or a doctor's appointment or arrived late at preschool—would never have used those words to describe me. "Unfit mothers" were drug addicts or women who neglected or abandoned their children outright. And yet he had let his lawyer use those words. The audacity and the cruelty of it were breathtaking. What had things come to?

Even though I dreaded every minute of the impending custody negotiation process, I was armed for battle. I was a tigress who would kill before letting another animal approach or abduct her cubs.

My lawyer began to prepare me for what steps we would need to take to satisfy a judge about my fitness as a mother. Lists of all the functions I regularly performed for my children. School records and records of inoculations. I might need a few character witnesses. And of course, I was to expect to incur some sizable legal fees.

Could it get any worse, I thought? I was sick to my stomach.

And then the miracle happened, as miracles sometimes do when I most need one. Or maybe it just felt like a miracle in the guise of a very wise therapist. Rather than listening and offering gentle suggestions as she usually did, this soft-spoken Argentine woman spoke up with uncharacteristic firmness.

"If there's one thing I can tell you, it's this: You must—*must*—remove the lawyers from any discussions regarding the children. Anything having to do with arrangements regarding the children must be worked out by you and their father alone. *No one else* can make those decisions. You can consult me, the child psychologist, whomever you need to consult throughout the process. But the decisions must be yours alone—yours and their father's.

"I have seen what can happen when these issues are settled in a courtroom," she continued. "Families are destroyed. Children are traumatized. It's a heartbreak. The only ones who benefit are the lawyers."

"But how could we possibly negotiate anything as complicated as a custodial access agreement?" I asked. "I just don't think we're capable. . . . "

"No one is better qualified to decide what is best for your children than the two of you, their parents. Think of it. You two know them best and know what's going to be best for them. No one else—and certainly not a judge or a lawyer."

What she was asking was more than overwhelming—it was impossible. Things had been so contentious between us for so many months now, I dreaded the thought of trying to speak to Bill directly about anything.

"But how?" I asked. "We can't even be in the same room any more without fighting."

"Start with a cup of coffee," she answered.

It was not something I wanted to do. But this admonition had come from someone I trusted intensely. There seemed to be little choice. If I was a tigress protecting my cubs, I had to go to any lengths.

Bill agreed to meet me at the local diner where we had eaten with the children many times. Clearly startled to receive my phone call, Bill had given brusque, one-word replies to my suggestions that we meet to discuss the children. Across the booth, his face was now as hard as I had ever seen it, encased in suspicion and hostility. It seemed surreal. Here we were practically in arm-to-arm combat, surrounded by people chatting, enjoying breakfast, and going about their everyday lives. At least it would force us to keep our voices down, should things erupt as they sometimes did.

We ordered coffee. I had thought long and hard about what to say and how to present this novel concept that we write and negotiate a custody agreement alone, without lawyers to guide us. But in the end the words were not important—not how clear I sounded, how organized my thoughts, how much or how little confidence I seemed to exude in this delicate discussion. What was important was the message, nothing more. This was about our children.

"No one knows those boys, no one loves them and understands them, as you and I do. I don't want a judge telling us how to raise them. I don't think you do either. We have to do this ourselves. Without the lawyers," I said.

Bill eyed me with suspicion. I had been married to this man long enough to be able to read his thoughts. What was I up to? Was this a manipulation to somehow give me the advantage?

I continued. "If it's just you and me writing that agreement—deciding when they come and go, how they live, what's best for them—it's the only way we can protect them from whatever damage a divorce is going to do to them. That has to be our overriding goal."

Like a momentary ray of sunlight piercing a thick storm cloud, Bill's expression softened and he nodded, though only slightly. "Yes," he said. For just a moment I could see the graduate school student who took long bike rides with me and had once been my best friend.

It was his turn to speak, and the hostility was gone from his voice. "I've thought about this a lot," he said. "You don't know how much I want to keep the boys completely separate from all this. Keep them in a kind of a bubble, completely removed. Or . . . you know how in the ancient synagogues they used to keep a fence around the Torah, to keep it protected? That's what I want to do for those boys. Put a fence around them."

"Yes," I said.

"And there's something else, too," Bill said. "It's important that these discussions be completely unrelated to any financial or property decisions. There can't be any quid pro quo between money and my access to the children."

This had not even occurred to me. It sickened me to think that parents might use their children in this way, as bargaining tools to gain financial advantage. Perhaps his lawyer had warned him.

"Of course," I said. And we began.

"Let's start with the weekends," I said. "I agree that every other weekend is the way it's usually done. But they're still so little. Maybe just for now we should split every weekend, so they don't have to be away from either of us for more than a day at a time. Then later—in six months or a year, maybe—we can go to alternating weekends. . . ."

The cups of coffee were refilled several times. Our voices remained calm and businesslike. We agreed to each make a list of what we saw as all the issues—weekends, vacations, medical decisions—and work them out on the phone, one by one. We would continue the next day.

"There's one more thing I need to say to you," I said, as Bill pulled out his wallet to pay the check. He looked at me, and the storm clouds were back.

"I will never believe," I said, speaking slowly and carefully, "that you would ever, ever—that you did ever—call me an unfit mother."

He stared at me, unmoving. His face was hard, but not hard enough to conceal a shadow that fell across his eyes. Was it a shadow of remorse? This time I could not tell.

Almost imperceptibly, he moved his head side to side: "No." Then he was gone.

It took many months. The process was not easy. We seemed to begin every issue in diametric opposition to each other. He wanted the boys for at least half of every summer; I wanted their maximum time away from me to be a week while they were young, maybe two weeks when they became teenagers. I wanted his weekends with them to begin Saturday morning and end at five o'clock in the evening on Sunday; he argued that his weekend should begin immediately after school on Fridays and extend to the start of school on Monday mornings. Many times the conversations became brittle. Emotions surfaced.

Three factors were always in play, each working against each other: The first was the time Bill wanted with these children he adored. The second was the time I wanted with these children I adored, along with my absolute certainty that nobody, not even Bill, could take care of them as well as I could. Then came a third factor: what was best for our sons' lives. Among these three forces was a natural tension that very often led to opposing solutions. Sometimes we reached an impasse. When this happened, we went back to my therapist's words.

"Keep in mind, in every discussion, in every conflict, this is not about 'what you get.' And it is not about 'what he gets.' This is about *what is best for the children*. That must be your guiding principle in every situation. Even if the solution feels uncomfortable to either of you, you must remember that this is not about either of you. It is about *them*. It is about giving *them* the best lives you can give them."

We concluded that what would make the children happiest was to wake up on Saturday mornings and not immediately have to run out to their father's house on alternate weekends but to be able to have their lazy mornings watching cartoons in their pajamas as usual. So I agreed that the "custodial access weekends" would begin Friday evenings just before dinner. We talked about Sunday evenings, those difficult times when the anxieties of the upcoming school week always seemed to creep back into our children's lives and behavior. We agreed they would come home to their "primary residence"— my house—by Sunday at five o'clock in the evening. This would give them plenty of time to prepare for Monday morning, both practically and emotionally.

The discussions went on and on, at times seeming interminable. Who would choose the pediatrician, the orthodontist? What happened if a child needed therapy—who decided, and who paid? What about grandparents? We both agreed we wanted the children to have plentiful and ready access to all of their grand-parents—but on "whose time" would the visits occur? What about religious holidays?

We knew of other divorcing parents who, when making custodial arrangements, left a good many decisions up to the children themselves. Sometimes a child could even decide with which parent he wished to live. This we deliberately would not allow. We would present to our children the guidelines that would govern their comings and goings as a fait accompli. The times they spent with their father, or with their mother, would be carved in stone. Our intention was to protect our children from the emotional torture of ever having to choose between parents—whether for a Saturday, a vacation, or their entire lives.

When we were finished, we sent my lawyer a thick document detailing what we had agreed, instructing him to create a legal agreement. Our attorneys reviewed what we had decided; and they did at times point out certain things we had omitted or left vague. But our instructions to them were clear. First, the decisions we had reached were final, and not up for discussion. Second, as Bill had suggested, none of this would be in any way connected to or contingent upon any other agreement we would later develop regarding finances or property. This would be a stand-alone document, separate and protected. As though in a bubble, or surrounded by a fence.

That was over a decade ago. The children have now reached their teen years and beyond. How did these children of a painful, difficult divorce turn out? I can say this unequivocally: that the way we raised them as children who belonged to two separate homes, governed by the agreement that we tediously began to hammer out over that long-ago cup of coffee, is the one thing, in my life at least, I can call an unqualified success. Our three boys grew up confident and secure in two different, peaceful, loving homes. Never having had to choose between their parents, they have close, comfortable relationships with both their father and me. They get along well with each other and with friends. There have been girlfriends, some long-term. All three have excelled in school, with the two oldest attending Ivy League colleges. The fact that their lives were not cradled in wall-to-wall comfort, that they had extra responsibilities—remembering in which house their schoolbooks were left, helping their mother shoulder difficult household chores, preparing their week's assignments while keeping in mind in which house they would be spending the night—only made them more capable and mature than a good many of their peers. Mostly, I believe that they are truly secure—as only children with reliable, mature, and loving parents can be.

Losing It

It had to be the lowest point in my whole miserable divorce.

I was hunched on the floor of my bedroom, sobbing. Ten days before I was to close on a new house, Bill had outmaneuvered me in a legal wrangle. Now that the Custodial and Residential Access Agreement had been executed, we were deep into financial settlement matters. As a negotiation tactic for some provision he wanted, he had legally managed to freeze the funds that were earmarked for the purchase of my new house. The boys and I had been temporarily living in a rented house for three months since selling our old house—the "marital home"—until we could move to a new permanent home. The rental lease contained a stiff penalty for every day we remained past a promised vacating date. If I defaulted on the purchase of the new house—for example, due to not having access to funds required at closing—I would lose my down payment and our new home.

I had been snookered. Here I was, my back against the wall, literally and figuratively. Defeat, fear, powerlessness, and even—I'll admit it—downright hatred overtook me completely. In the rush of hot emotion, all reason was swept away. The logical thought that I would simply call my lawyer the next day to find out whether I had any recourse never occurred to me. At that moment, this was no longer a civil lawsuit, this was a knife fight—and I had been gored.

Practically crouched under my night table, I let out loud, racking sobs.

There was a timid knock on the door. David, my normally self-assured, confident twelve-year-old son, spoke in a voice with an uncharacteristic tremble. "Mom," he said, urgently, "Mom, what's wrong? Can I come in?"

I had tried so hard, at the bad moments, to keep my tears hidden from the children. But this time, control was gone.

"No," I choked, still unable to stop crying. "Not now."

Even in my distressed state, I knew that this was the last thing David needed to see or hear. Not much time had passed since that most awful day of all, the day we told the children their father would be moving out. The day David had silently laid his forehead on the kitchen table for a few long moments, then, blank faced, announced he was going upstairs to watch television. When I went up after him, he wouldn't talk, just stared at the screen. Hadn't we caused them enough pain?

The door opened a crack. "Mom, please!" he said, and

this time his voice was louder and more urgent. "What's wrong? What happened?" His face peered through the door at me and became panicked when he saw me crouched on the floor. "Mom! What happened?"

His worried look made me cry all the more. "Please, David, not now," I sputtered. "It's just this divorce. Your father . . . your father is . . . " I couldn't stop the words spilling out. Inside my head I heard what I felt at this moment: That his father was trying to destroy me. That he would destroy me, would leave us homeless.

Abruptly, my words stopped. Saying this out loud, I knew, would be the cardinal sin. But it was too late. David put one finger to each eye, the way he did when trying not to let anyone see him cry. He retreated and closed the door with a quiet click. Had he heard my thoughts?

From the other side of the door, his younger brother was pleading with him. "David, what is it?" Robert's ten-year-old voice was uncharacteristically urgent and, at the same time, terrified. His brother didn't answer, and Robert persisted. "David, tell me! I have a right to know! Tell me what's wrong!"

Through the closed door, I could picture what must be fear on Robert's normally sunny, sweet face. The effect was like an overturned ice bucket; it brought me to my senses. I could not do this to my sons. No matter what was going on in the divorce, these little boys had to be protected.

I didn't have to imagine the impact of my sobs upon my children. I knew it. Long ago, during my mother's distraught days and months after my father moved out,

I had no name for that ugly, desolate feeling of witnessing her emotional breakdowns. It felt like there was a
huge hole in the ground that I could fall through at any
moment, down into a deep, black chasm. Not that my
mother hadn't tried to keep it from us as well; she tried
hard—or thought she did. She did this by keeping
secrets. Many, many secrets.

But the secrets only made it worse. I could sense my
mother's moods, from moment to moment, even
through closed doors. From when I was only six, then
seven, and then up through my teens, I could feel—and
seemed to absorb—my mother's pain and fear as though
they were my own.

I knew everything. I just knew. I was acutely aware of
every expression on my mother's face, every quiver in her
voice, the droop of her shoulders. I could sense my
mother's mood in the electric charge in the air, even
when returning home to an empty apartment. Sometimes
the telephone in my mother's bedroom jangled with
urgent portent; other times, it rang a soft greeting. I
watched and sensed and listened behind closed doors.
Although I couldn't make out her words on the telephone, the sound of her voice told me everything. When
my mother, about to leave her second failing marriage,
became accidentally pregnant, she wouldn't break the
news to us for another five months. But I sensed it, knew
it with absolute certainty, only days after she had learned
of it herself. Ten years old, I carried the secret inside
me—for if my mother was keeping her pregnancy from
me, I reasoned it must have been a truly terrible secret. I
worried and fretted and prayed that it wasn't so. The

sister that was born of that pregnancy was to become one of the greatest joys of my childhood, and in later years, my best friend. But in those days, when I searched my mother's face and listened for her sobs through closed doors, I could only imagine what true terrors lay in this and all the other unspoken secrets.

No. I would not do this to my boys. I wouldn't burden them with my pain or my fears. But keeping it from them would do no good either. It was tricky. Honesty was called for—but how much?

I stood up and grabbing a few tissues, opened the door. They had disappeared down the hall. "Guys, come in here a minute." How did I manage to keep my voice so normal? Somehow I did.

Two frightened small faces appeared. David's wore a dark cloud of mistrust.

"Listen, guys, I'm okay, really," I said. I opened the door wide, "Come in, both of you. I want to tell you what happened," I said, drying my eyes.

First, I would make my voice normal, back to my usual calm, in-charge sound. The boys came in quietly. There was still hesitation in David's eyes and worry in Robert's.

I didn't try to hide the fact that my eyes were red. "You know I've been crying," I said. "I'll tell you why. But first I want you guys to know that I'm okay, really."

Then, keeping it as simple as I could, I explained. That this divorce that we were going through was a sad and difficult thing. That it was really hard for me and their dad, ending our marriage, moving, all that. That in going through this divorce, sometimes their dad and I had fights, but we were working them out. That sometimes I felt so bad it made me cry. But that was not such a bad thing at all because I usually felt better after crying. That their dad and I had made a strict and solemn promise that no matter what happened, we would both take as good care of our boys as we always had. Working out details about money and the move could be complicated and hard. Sometimes we got angry. But it was nothing we couldn't solve.

"I know it was probably scary to hear me cry like that," I said. "But you know, that happens to me sometimes. Not too often. The important thing is that you know I'm really all right, and we're all okay."

I knew that the words didn't really matter at all. It was the sound of my voice that mattered. I didn't try to sound cheerful—they would know it was fake. But I kept my voice as level and normal sounding as possible.

"One more thing," I said. "If there's anything you want to know, I want you to ask me. I can't promise I'll answer you completely—some things are private. But I won't lie to you."

Maybe it was the sound of my own steady voice that made me feel, just for that moment, a little calmer myself. Someone was in charge here. We would be all right.

The boys had relief on their faces but also something else. David, keeping his eyes down, looked a twinge more mature. Robert's face was calm but just a shade less sunny. I reached for them and hugged them, one at a time.

"Mom, you forgot about our milk and cookies," Robert said quietly.

"Yes, and I forgot something else. I meant to tell you I

bought Mallomars today. Come, let's go to the kitchen."
Barefoot and in their pajamas, the boys led the way
downstairs.

And life went on. The next morning, I called my
lawyer, who filed an emergency motion with the court to
have the funds released. Nine days later, I closed on our
new home.

"You Are Your Future"

"**Y**ou realize, of course" said the massage therapist, "that seventy-five percent of all divorced women end up living below the poverty line. Let me tell you what happened to me. . . . " Her story continued for the next fifty-five minutes, complete with tales of her unpaid medical bills and unfair child support judgment. "Just wait, you'll see," she finished up.

And this was where I had supposedly come for one hour of relaxation from the stress of my impending divorce.

What if she's right? I thought. I tried to quell a rising sense of panic. The fact that our marital net worth should be enough for both of us didn't seem to matter. She was right. I would be left with nothing.

I had not worked in a full-time job for years. After my first son, David, was born, I left my job as a corporate lending officer in New York City. With that, I exchanged the security of earning my own paycheck for the satisfaction of being home with my baby. But it was more than satisfaction; rather, it felt like compulsion, as though I had no choice. At the same time, not going back to Bankers Trust Company was about the easiest decision I ever made. I had become completely unenamored with the life of a corporate banker, which regularly included highlights such as flying to Pittsburgh to convince prospects that a Bankers Trust Letter of Credit at prime plus fifty basis points was preferable to a Chase Letter of Credit.

And yet, resigning from the bank meant abandoning a resolution I had made long ago. Throughout my childhood, my divorced mother's financial struggles dominated both my awake and dreaming life. "I will never, never be financially dependent on a man," I had vowed at twelve, and then again at sixteen, and many times after that. The vow held its own power, fueled sometimes by anger at a father who paid meager child support, sometimes by fear and worry. There were other times, too, particularly during my early college years, when I was energized with a heady sense of my burgeoning talents, and my eagerness to take on the world.

Of course, it was the fact that Bill earned enough money to support our family that allowed me to surrender to that tidal wave urge to mother. Not many other women even had that choice. Certainly my divorced mother had not, with her full-time job as a sales rep for a food distribution company, along with her second job, teaching nursing skills in an upper Manhattan vocational school three evenings per week and all day Saturdays. The school was in a tough neighborhood, and I was always glad when she returned to our apartment at ten o'clock in the evening to the dinner I had cooked and left covered in aluminum foil. Only once was she mugged in an elevator on 110th Street. She had used her teacher's voice to instruct the young man with the switchblade to yes, take the money from her wallet, but the prescription glasses would be of no use to him and to please leave them behind. It became more difficult for me after that, as I cleaned the kitchen after making dinner for my brothers and baby sister, waiting for that sound of the elevator door to slam open on our landing at night.

I will have a real *job,* I would think, wiping the counters—*a job that makes lots of money. I'm going to get to the top, I'll be so successful that I will earn all the money I could ever need, plus more. I'll never have to wait for a child support check or borrow an extra hundred dollars from a friend, like mom does from time to time.* With those thoughts always somewhere in mind, I would settle at the kitchen table with my social studies or biology textbooks and work without stopping, listening for the sound of the elevator door on the landing.

But that long-ago vow knew nothing of the smell of my newborn's silky head or the way my entire body rose up in a kind of fire when he cried heartbreaking sobs at three o'clock in the morning. I could no sooner leave this boy in a housekeeper's care than go for a walk while leaving one of my limbs at home. So I told my boss at the bank that I wouldn't be coming back from maternity leave. He wasn't surprised; he had heard it before.

I was supremely grateful that Bill earned enough

money for the two of us. What a blessed relief not to rush to a train to New York City each morning but instead to surrender to the powerful instinct to breast-feed my son. Leaving the baby with Bill two evenings a month, I took writing workshops and developed as a writer. How lucky I was not to be required to earn money of my own.

Or so I thought.

Sitting in a lawyer's office thirteen years later, with a marriage in shambles, I faced the total collapse of my family life along with an angry ex-husband determined to make me pay good hard dollars for not wanting the marriage any longer. From the outset, he made it clear that he fully intended to be the one to retain most, if not all, of our assets. "I'm going to be very wealthy again one day," he said. "And when you end up with nothing, don't come looking to me."

The pronouncement stayed with me, irrefutable, immutable. It haunted me like the curse of the evil fairy who appears uninvited at Sleeping Beauty's christening, vowing that the baby will one day prick her finger on a spindle and die.

What would happen to me? What were my career prospects, now that I had not held a real job in so many years? Yes, it had been a good thing to be home and available all that time with what by now were three young sons. Or had it? And what if I still were forging ahead in a career at the bank? Would I perhaps have been promoted to vice president by now? How much would I be earning? I could even imagine that monthly pay stub—how it would look on its two-part form.

If I did have to look for a job now, what was I qualified

for? What kind of career could I show for myself after thirteen years of "staying home to raise my children"? And wouldn't the world always insist on seeing my running the financial side of Bill's business as little more than "working for my husband"—as Bill himself did?

From a modest beginning, Bill had built a business developing commercial real estate, gradually acquiring more properties over the years of our marriage. The business had done very well due to a continually escalating real estate market. It also prospered due to the fact that Bill was married to a woman with sophisticated financial skills and banking experience, who eagerly plunged into supporting the family business. Beginning with my first maternity leave, I spent many hours initially in our home office, then alongside Bill in space we rented in an office building in town, securing construction loans, filing tax and financial reports, reconciling and billing common area charges, and buying our computer and accounting software. Eventually I hired office support staff while continuing to oversee our financial operations. I was able to keep flexible hours, which enabled me to drop off Robert at preschool and leave the office before David got home from kindergarten. Not only did this arrangement make enormous financial sense, but it also allowed me to use my skills and intellect in a way that provided great relief from "Mommy and Me" brain drain. At the same time, it always added an additional troubling aspect to our marriage. Bill always spoke of the business as his alone, referring to my contribution as merely "helping him in his business." Clearly I didn't understand then how much Bill needed some purview for which he alone could claim credit. Instead, I frequently expressed my resentment at his failure to show sufficient appreciation for the long hours I devoted to the business. When pressed, he would admit to me that of course what I did was very helpful. Nevertheless, he always referred to it as "my real estate business," never "ours." When the divorce discussions began, it was clear that this perspective had crystallized into a firm legal position.

Despite attempts to reassure myself, it was terror I faced on the day I sat across the desk from a young lawyer named Mark Weingarten. I was surprised to discover how youthful and fresh-faced the lawyer—who had been recommended to me as someone particularly experienced in real estate valuations and partnership dissolutions—was. With wire-rimmed glasses and rosy cheeks, he looked barely thirty, if that. And here I was, in my forties with three children, trying to stave off panic by getting an expert assessment of how much our real estate was worth and how much I might expect to receive as a settlement.

These were critical, heart-stopping issues for me. They would make the difference, I thought, between having the ability to remain in our house with my three young children—my oldest was not yet even ten—or to move to an apartment somewhere with bunk beds crammed into one bedroom and a pull-out sofa in the living room for me, like the one my mother had slept in years ago. It would mean the difference, I imagined, between planning my children's birthday parties or letting someone else raise them while I commuted to a miserable banking job in the city.

Since the day Bill moved out, all my old memories of growing up in financial insecurity had come flooding back in images that were crisp and searing. The day I had been forced to drop my sister Karyn off, red-faced and screaming, at a day care center because I had to end my summer taking care of her to begin my junior year of high school. Grocery shopping with my mother at Gristedes and watching her put items back from the conveyor because the total exceeded the money she had. Keeping my eyes down, so she could not see that I had spotted the food stamps hidden in her purse. Would this be my children's lives now?

And what about me? "Go get a job; go be useful!" Bill had thrown at me during one of our angry exchanges about money soon after our separation. Even though I knew it was precipitated by bitter emotion, that comment wounded me deeply. So caring for his three young children was not useful? My nights became consumed with worry over the imagined prospect of having to turn my forlorn sons over to distracted day care workers who would not hide their annoyance when I picked the boys up late due to a broken-down Metro North train.

In the light of morning, I would try to shake away the nightmare images. We lived a comfortable life in the suburbs. Bill would never let his sons go wanting. Our financial reality today could not possibly lead to a return to all that. Or could it?

Mark Weingarten spoke calmly, with a thorough knowledge that his young face belied. He didn't sugarcoat the facts, but they weren't terrible, either. Yes, I had a partnership interest in the real estate—the fact that I had worked in the business was not the deciding factor; community property laws were. The challenge would be how my ex-husband could finance a buyout. If he could not, perhaps I should consider remaining a financial partner—something I knew Bill would resist at all costs. With anxiety in my voice, I threw emotion-fueled questions at him that he answered with simple, legal facts. "How will the properties be valued, and by whom?" I asked, remembering the evil curse. "What if my husband tries to cheat me? How will I know? Then what would I do? You have to know how important this is," I said to him, tension in my voice. "This is everything. This is my future."

Then Mark did a very unlawyerly thing. He brought his hands together and leaned forward on the desk. Fixing his wire-rimmed eyes on me, he spoke with authority.

"No, Jessica," he said. "You are your future. Everything you are, all your talents that brought you to where you are, all your abilities, your knowledge, your courage. Everything you have accomplished that has made you what you are right now—that's your future, Jessica. Not the real estate, not the money. You are your future and you must never forget that."

He was young, but I believed him.

After that, I became calmer. *Wait a minute,* I realized, thinking of the divorce negotiations that lay ahead of me. *I understand our business. I have financial skills. What I don't know about real estate valuations, I will learn—the same way I learned about the Romantic poets in college, aced advanced accounting in graduate school, and figured out how to design a spreadsheet on a computer for the first time. I can do this. I— we—would be all right.*

What followed was a long, drawn-out, contentious financial battle that ended up costing each of us in legal fees a good portion of those embattled assets. Despite Bill's early assurance that the business belonged to him alone, his lawyer presumably educated him soon enough that marital property laws stipulated that assets acquired during the term of a marriage are regarded as jointly owned, regardless of which spouse claims "ownership" of the business. The negotiations dragged on. Calling upon my banking knowledge, along with what I had learned about real estate from working in our business all those years, I was able to hold my own throughout the negotiations. When I became convinced that the appraiser Bill selected to value the assets to be divided in a settlement had undervalued those assets, I contested the appraisal by hiring an appraiser of my own.

Sometimes the biggest challenge was to keep my emotions from intruding on what I came to see as my new full-time job of getting divorced. For the most part, I succeeded in staying calm and clear-headed. Mark's assurances had helped. So did the almost clear sound of the ticking taxi meter every time I picked up the phone to call my accountant or divorce attorney.

Eventually we came to a settlement. If it wasn't as financially generous as I had originally hoped, I decided that it was acceptable. I received some cash to put away for retirement, as well as a small financial safety net while I figured out my next steps. Bill became the sole owner of the real estate properties. As far as I was concerned, I had held up my end. And I would have enough.

I did have to sell our house and move to a much smaller one in a new town. But my sons had their birthday parties there, and I came to love that small house, filled with laughter and the clutter of three growing boys, more than any house I had ever lived in before. When my sons were in school, I began writing business stories, for which I was paid $75 each, for a local newspaper. Then another local newspaper asked me if I could write and edit special sections for $100 a page. They would teach me Quark, the newspaper layout software. To seek out ideas for business stories I began attending chamber of commerce and other networking gatherings. The executive director of my local chamber offered me a free membership in exchange for writing a member profile in each monthly newsletter.

Finally, at a networking meeting one bitterly cold February evening, when I resisted the urge to stay home where it was warm, the publisher of a local newspaper group approached me with a glass of white wine in hand. "We need an editor for a new monthly business publication we're about to launch," he said. "You'd be perfect. If you're interested, call me tomorrow morning," he said, handing me his card.

One challenge followed another, one stumble, and one success—until I eventually began a home-based business of my own as a writer and PR consultant. I was in my home office—although steadily working—when my sons came home from school. Interested mostly in their own after-school Wiffle Ball games or homework, they seldom interrupted me, except to ask for an occasional five dollars for Planet Pizza down the road. Even if they didn't see me until dinner time, I was glad that they knew that the house was not empty, my car was in the garage, and dinner—even though it might consist of nothing more than chicken nuggets and pasta thrown together in a rush—would be served well in time for Boy Scouts or jazz band practice at a kitchen table set for four.

Today my life is filled with everything I could ever have wanted or imagined for myself and more. The real estate buyout was put aside for my retirement and to fund a long-term care policy, should I ever need full-time care. Other than that, I earn my own living. I write, I teach writing, and regularly record commentaries that air on my local National Public Radio station. Best of all, I spend every day doing what I love—none of which has anything to do with financial management, banking, or real estate.

I think often of Mark Weingarten, and what he said to me that day. I think of his words, so wise for someone so young. I think of them somewhat like that last good fairy who arrives at Sleeping Beauty's christening who, although she cannot undo the evil curse, pronounces that the young princess will not die after all, but only fall into a gentle sleep from which she will one day joyfully awaken.

Bill did become quite wealthy after our divorce. Real estate values took off, and all the properties, along with the new ones he acquired, became fully rented. He bought a Jaguar, takes international trips several times a year, and skis in Aspen. He bought an expensive house and had it professionally decorated. Most important, and to my and my sons' good fortune, he is able to pay for our children's college.

I do none of these things. The monthly fuel bill and medical insurance can be a stretch; I take vacations with my children at home. When friends comment on the vast difference between my former husband's and my lifestyles, what I like to tell them is this: Yes, he ended up with most of the money. And I ended up rich.

Something About Guilt

"You've got a sad little boy there," said the child psychologist from his leather chair, peering at Bill and me over his pipe.

Yes, Robert was sad. This was something we already knew. But hearing the words from this stranger who the week before had spent forty-five minutes with our nine-year-old son brought on a sickening new wave of guilt. It was a feeling that had become all too familiar.

Robert had been looking downcast since his father had moved to a rental house less than two miles away. We had done everything possible to soften the blow, like keeping the children on an established routine and furnishing their new rooms in Bill's house with the familiar Sesame Street bedding, Little League trophies, and lots of LEGOs. Although our financial and legal battles were well underway and far from resolved, Bill and I had kept the children out of it.

The boys had been surprisingly compliant about their new routine. If they didn't exactly like the back and forth—and why would they?—at least their lives were orderly and predictable. But still, Robert was sad. Until then, he had been the most fun-loving and sociable of the three—sunny is how most people described him. Now he seemed to be spending more time than usual engrossed in a TV show or video game. Sometimes I caught him teary-eyed at bedtime. Tucking him into bed one night, I asked him what seemed to be the matter. Hadn't we done everything possible to convince him that his parents both still loved him and would always be in his life? "Yes, but when I'm with you, I miss Dad. And when I'm with Dad, I miss you," he answered. There was nothing I could say to this, only stroke back his curls and kiss him goodnight.

At times like this, guilt would resurface, like a sea monster with giant, punishing claws. I knew I was doing the right thing to go ahead with the divorce. But in my weaker moments, I would find myself second-guessing. *Couldn't I have been a better wife, so we could have stayed married and our sons could have had a two-parent home? Couldn't we have tried one more time?* All I had to do was think back on the years, the endless couples counseling and discussions, the dogged unhappiness, and the answer that always came back was a resounding no.

In those early months after separating, I learned to expect those occasional reminders of guilt. Sometimes they were the sea monster, at other times merely annoying pangs, like an intrusive neighbor who continually finds excuses to ring the doorbell. I could resist the barrage of blame from the naysayers and the Dr. Judith Wallersteins of the world. But I was no match for one of my sons trying to maintain big-boy composure with fingers pressed against eyelids to suppress tears.

This was where reason and emotion diverged. Try as I might to reassure myself I was doing the right thing or to soak up encouragement from friends and professionals, I couldn't stop myself from regretting the simple fact that I had participated in depriving my children of a "stable" home with two parents. The long chats that Bill had with the boys every night at bedtime would now take place only on Tuesday nights and every other weekend. There was a loss. That was undeniable.

Of the three children, Robert was the only one to be visibly mourning. Bill and I consulted a child psychologist who had recommended we bring our son to see him.

When we broached the idea, Robert was resistant. "I don't know what I would talk about," he said. But Bill and I persisted. "How about this?" I said. "Just go once. If you don't like it, we promise you absolutely don't have to go back." We gave him a choice of two that had been referred to us—a young guy who had toys and games in his office, and who was supposedly fun and popular with children, or someone much older, with a lot more experience and training. With great reluctance, Robert agreed to go once, opting for the younger one. As it turned out, the younger psychologist was booked for several weeks, so we ended up bringing Robert to the snowy-haired sage with the leather volume–lined office and not a single toy in sight.

Despite slightly red eyes, a hint of Robert's humor returned as he got in the car after his forty-five minute session. "If that was the young, cool guy, I'd hate to see the older one," he muttered, and I couldn't help a smile. Did it help? "Nope." Want to go back? "No way."

He was right. Nothing was going to repair the tear in the cozy, cushioned family unit that Robert had known until then. No psychotherapy or counseling was going to fix this.

Only once did one of my children attempt to play the guilt card. It was a Sunday evening, after the boys returned from their weekend with Bill, and it was obvious that my oldest, twelve-year-old David, was rushing through dinner. Only minutes after I sat down after serving everyone else, David asked to be excused. I looked at the clock; there was still plenty of time before the start of *The Simpsons,* a TV show around which his life, along with that of his entire seventh grade class, seemed to revolve these days.

"Oh, honey, please stay at the table a little longer. I don't get the chance to have dinner with you guys that often, don't forget. I really want to have this time with you."

"Whose fault is that?" David murmured, shooting me a dark glance before quickly looking away.

"Meaning?" I shot back at him. I knew exactly what he meant, and it was like a knife in my gut.

"I mean, if you weren't getting a divorce, then you wouldn't have to miss us when we're not here . . . " he said, avoiding my eyes.

With a shaking hand, I put down my fork. My dinner had suddenly turned unappetizing.

He was right, of course. But I had been warned by my

kind friend Cis, with all her eighty-plus-year-old wisdom, never to let children manipulate with guilt. "Be very watchful for this. It gives them too much power, and it's ultimately very harmful to them," she had said.

Until this moment, it had never happened. What would Cis tell me to do? I couldn't let David get away with that comment. But I could hardly punish him for expressing his feelings, could I?

My voice became very quiet. "David, you know how bad I feel about the fact your dad and I are getting divorced. And what you just said was so hurtful to me, I don't even want to be around you any more. So go, you're excused."

That was all. David left the table. His brothers, who had been silently looking down at their plates, soon finished eating and followed him. I stood up and began to clear off the table, wiping the plate with my uneaten dinner into the trash. I had rarely felt so low and never so defeated. I felt like a total failure.

It turned out to be the first and last recrimination I was ever to hear from any of my sons. But even without being reminded, the low, somber drumbeat of guilt would regularly reappear like the beat of Edgar Allen Poe's "Telltale Heart." I often found myself falling into a subconscious pattern called "Making It Up to the Children." Having failed to grant them a perfect, unbroken home, I resolved to do everything I could to make their lives as easy as possible. I would cater to their every desire before they even knew they wanted anything, supply them with new shoes and clothes before the old ones were outgrown. I ran to six different toy stores until I was able to snag the coveted, recently released action toys that were just being unpacked from their shipping boxes. Mealtimes, I was the classic short-order-cook mom. Every child had a different meal that contained only that child's special favorite. On school mornings, breakfast became hectic as I made cheese ravioli for David, grilled cheese with cheddar for Robert, grilled cheese with American for Alex. The housekeeper we had been able to afford when I was married was long gone, so laundry and cleaning fell to me after the boys went to sleep. When my mother suggested that I let the boys help me with a few household chores, I resisted. Hadn't my sons suffered enough, to be asked to empty wastebaskets, too? No, I would handle it myself. Let them be children.

My new therapist firmly pointed out the error of this thinking. "Take it from me, I've seen a good many adults who, as children, had far more damage ultimately done to them by overindulgence than by deprivation," he said. In no uncertain terms, he gave me marching orders. "Give those boys jobs to do. Get them to help."

I hated every bit of the idea. Why should I make my sons responsible for the fact that I had a household to handle on my own, when they clearly had played no role in making that decision? How could I possibly inflict upon my sons what I remembered from my own childhood, when my distraught divorced mother had relied upon me to handle far more household responsibilities than any child should have been given? But with great reluctance—and only because the last thing I wanted to do was to inflict more damage on my already-suffering children—I decided to give it a try.

Several days later, I dumped a large basket of clean wash

onto my bed and called the three boys into my room.

"I'm going to teach you guys to fold and sort laundry. I can't do it all myself and really need your help," I said. The three of them looked at me, dubious.

As usual, David was the first to speak up. "Mom, does it have to be now? *The Simpsons* starts soon and then *Malcolm in the Middle.*"

"No problem. I'll turn on the TV in here, and you can watch while we fold." There was no further objection.

David's job was to fold T-shirts and undershirts, a task he quickly caught onto after two demonstrations. Alex, the youngest and only six, had only to match up socks, after which Robert rolled them up and tossed them into the laundry basket. I folded pajamas, underwear, and the rest.

This became our biweekly routine. As long as the TV was left on so not a moment of their prebedtime shows was missed, the boys didn't issue a single protest. Despite an occasional stall in the folding during a Mets game when the boys had to stop to watch an important at bat, the four of us made short work of the laundry. It was a revelation to me how quickly a huge basket of newly washed clothes could be dispatched this way. Even better was the unexpected fun of watching the boys cheerfully jockey for prime TV-viewing position, or watching Robert lob sock rolls through the air into the empty laundry basket, while his brothers tried to jinx his throws.

After that, I gave each boy a job of his own. David's responsibility was to empty the dishwasher each morning before breakfast. David was an early riser, and his predawn clatter of dishes being put away downstairs often preceded the buzz of my alarm clock. Robert emptied wastebaskets and took out the garbage twice a week, although never without being reminded. Alex set the table and filled water glasses at dinner. When they finished eating, the three of them promptly cleared away their dishes and put them in the dishwasher. Although the boys still tended to finish eating while I was still halfway through, I usually had the pleasure of finishing my own dinner at a table that had been almost entirely cleaned off.

Among the many surprises was how little the boys complained or protested about their new chores. If anything, they seemed to stand a little taller when I thanked them for being so helpful. "What would I do without you guys?" I told them, catching them on their way out of the room for a quick kiss on each cheek. "You're the best!"

One night, several months after Robert's one and only visit to the child psychologist, I stepped into his dark room to put some clean clothes in his drawer. Robert was lying in bed, still awake. On an impulse, I came over and sat down next to him on his bed. "Can I hang out with you here a little while?" I asked. "Sure," he said and moved over to let me lie alongside him.

"Did I ever tell you the story about when my grandmother fell off a sled when she was a little girl in Russia?" I asked.

"Was your grandmother really from Russia?" he asked. "You never told me."

"Siberia. Well, the Ukraine actually. But it must have

been a lot like Siberia because it was always snowing." I then proceeded to tell him the story of how after a long trip by horse-drawn sled, her family had to go back to look for my four-year-old grandmother after failing for miles to notice that she was missing. When they retrieved her from the snow and got her back home, they warmed her up by putting her in the oven—or so the story went.

As I got up to leave, Robert moved closer toward me. "Wait—don't go yet. Tell me about when your grandmother came to America." I hesitated—there was a kitchen to clean up downstairs and bills to pay. But instead, I stayed, searching for more stories, until we were both sleepy.

After that, Robert's and my nighttime talks became our routine. With the darkened room lit only from the hallway, we would talk about everything from how much his Ken Griffey Jr. rookie cards were worth, to the waffles and sausage they had inexplicably served for lunch in the school cafeteria that day. He explained to me how foursquare worked and the new oddly-named game of "frolf" that he played at day camp. He especially loved hearing stories that were about him when he was younger, like the time he had stitches in his scalp after capsizing in a tricycle race in his friend Eric's driveway, and how impressed the emergency room staff had been by the grit of this boy who had issued not a whimper, only a sharp intake of breath and a quickly uttered "Oh, man!" when the first needle hit his skin.

This went on for a year or more. Many times I ached to go downstairs, finish cleaning the kitchen, and drag myself into my own bed with a book. But whenever I was about to say a final goodnight, and Robert would turn toward me, snuggle a little closer, and say "Don't go yet!" I usually held out for just a little longer.

One day, I peered in and found Robert already asleep. Soon afterward, I realized that my sad little boy wasn't sad any more. Then came adolescence, and our night-time talks were over.

With Robert now off at college, his empty room holds a special poignancy for me. As I pause some evenings at his door, it occurs to me that those bedtime talks did more than comfort my sad son. They also helped to put my feelings of guilt to rest. I could not undo my mistakes. Nor could I erase my children's pain or reverse whatever damage had been done to them by their parents' divorce. All I could do—one day at a time, one bedtime at a time, one basketful of clean laundry at a time—was to build a life and a future for myself and my sons for which I could be proud—a future that I would never come to regret.

Anger Management

There were a million reasons not to go through divorce being angry. And another thousand slogans to go with them. Almost daily I tried to remind myself of them: Life is too short. Be grateful that my children are healthy. Anger consumes valuable energy better spent on more productive pursuits.

But none of these ridiculous slogans did me one bit of good as, with anger pouring out of me like lava from a volcano, I churned through the months after my husband moved out.

Some days it circulated inside me like an endless current of bile. Profanities I had never spoken aloud ran through my brain. Crying into my wine glass with my friend Donna, the ugly words broke out like little toads from the unkind girl's mouth in the Grimm's fairy tale. After the words spewed out, the anger remained. Donna just shook her head sadly and let me vent.

Donna was a particularly sympathetic friend who never seemed to lose patience with my tales of woe. But I slowly began to suspect that it wasn't so with all the others. After a while I began to detect eyes wandering. An interrupted "Shall we order?" or change of subject got me wondering whether that friend had been listening at all to the latest update in my endlessly gripping soap opera of misery. Regrettably, I did not realize then that what was endlessly fascinating to me was not so to my friends, even the most caring of them. Finally one day, my mother, who had less restraint than my tactful friends, burst out, "Jessica! Enough! I can't listen any more!" which abruptly stifled any further angry outpouring. For that day, anyway.

After that, it did occur to me that it couldn't have been too pleasant to listen to an angry woman rail on and on about that jerk she was once married to, about how he had the nerve to do this or that. But I couldn't help it. Only later, when my life had settled down and newly divorcing friends bent my ear with similar angry tirades did I fully realize, belatedly, how truly unsavory these kinds of one-sided conversations are.

That I was capable of such anger took me by surprise. *Who is this angry, bitter person?* I wondered. Hadn't Bill and I resolved, once the divorce became inevitable, that whatever lay ahead, we would do this in the most civil way? Hadn't we agreed to rise above anger or blame, to think only of the children?

Yes, but that was before events took over, and everything changed. Once the cruel realities of money and property and child support payments appeared, things took on an ugly urgency. Then divorce lawyers were added to the mix, skillfully stoking accusation-laden documents with the fiery private details of our breakup. We were off and running.

To get away from my anger, one gorgeous October when I didn't have the children I drove to Vermont for a three-day organized bicycling weekend. The autumn scenery and all that exercise would be good for me, I decided. Bicycling would raise the serotonin levels and lift my foul mood, not to mention burn calories. I would eat healthy, country breakfasts—nothing high-carb, only proteins and vegetables. I would go alone, yes, but once there I would meet other cyclists with whom it would be easy to hook up for casual country rides. And then there would be the gorgeous Vermont countryside. God's green earth and the brilliant autumn foliage would certainly heal me and rid me of all negative thoughts. I imagined myself peddling over the hills, not angry but calm, grateful that my body was healthy, and that my limbs were strong enough to take me up the steep hills and let me fly down the other side. The fresh air alone would be medicine for my bedraggled, beaten-up soul.

A group of about eighteen of us lodged in the Golden Stage Inn in Proctorsville, Vermont, a picturesque bed and breakfast with fragrant hand-stitched cotton quilts and old country furniture that appeared to have weathered decades. Seated in the dining room at tables of six, we introduced ourselves before being served gorgeous country meals of roast chicken, autumn vegetables, fresh-baked rolls, and homemade breads.

Each day, breakfast was fresh scones and waffles,

loaded with fruits and newly tapped Vermont maple syrup. During breakfast there was also a talk with safety instructions and directions for a choice of easy, moderate, and challenging rides. Then the guides would send us off on long daily rides, our bicycles packed with maps, clean and filled water bottles, and high-energy snacks should anyone feel faint. There was even a chase van loaded with cookies, bananas, water, and first aid, in which a weary rider could hitch a ride back to the Inn for a nice nap. It couldn't have been more perfect.

And I couldn't have been more miserable.

As usual, most of the group were couples. At my table at dinner the first night there was one middle-aged couple from Philadelphia who had taken this weekend to celebrate their thirty-fifth anniversary. There was also a group of three men—an older man and his two married sons—who had traveled from different states to meet up for a father-son bicycling weekend. Then there was me. Worn, hollow-eyed, and exhausted from the divorce. With all the consolation eating and wine drinking I had been doing during the upheaval at home, I felt fortunate that my bike shorts still fit—but just barely. I was a mess.

The first cool morning the others set out in their close-knit groups, leaving me to pedal the country roads alone a good part of the time. But this didn't bother me. It would give me time to think and take in the quiet. I breathed the clean air deeply, riding alongside wide expanses of rolling green land. The hills were studded with cattle so serene and perfect that they seemed about to burst forth with Ben & Jerry's Maple Walnut Ice

Cream. My bicycle whooshed through deep woods shaded with deep greens, rust, and gold. It was as peaceable a scene as I could imagine. And in my head, it was still there, like a drumbeat that just won't stop or a song that gets stuck in your head: *I hate him. He wants to destroy me. How can he do this?* It went on and on.

I imagined the anger pouring off me like tar, trailing behind in a hot, gluey swath. I vowed to think positive; I would try to imagine the tar of my anger coating the bumpy country roads and paths beneath me, leaving it smooth for the other bikers. But the more it poured off me, the more my unlimited supply seemed to remain. Had it been real tar, every dirt path in northeastern Vermont would have ended up paved to perfection.

I biked on through the hours and the miles, and the sun rose higher in the sky. By late afternoon, as the hot sun began cresting toward the horizon, I realized something new. I realized that sometimes there is no escaping from anger. It didn't fall off me like tar. No talking myself out of it, nor cheery and enlightened slogans, could make it go away. No amount of glorious foliage, no freshly baked bread or red wine, could change my angry mood. Taking myself to the most peaceful spot on earth could not quiet the torrents of fear and fury inside me. I was still angry. The only difference was, I was now angry while surrounded by prettier scenery.

There was nothing for me to do with my anger but to let it run its course. By the end of the day's ride, I had let go of all those silly homilies about how anger hurts oneself more than the object of one's anger, how gratitude should replace grousing. I gave up trying to think myself out of anger. What I would do with all that still burning anger, I had no idea.

I learned something else about anger, too. As the sun slipped toward the golden brown horizon, with the first hint of autumn chill, a new feeling—a deep sense of grief—was stirred up inside me. I realized then how much easier it is to be angry than to feel the simple, searing pain of regret. So much had been lost with the dismantling of that troubled, yes, but sweet family. My children. My husband. We had tried so hard. Anger was the useful lubricant that salved the underlying wound. This sadness was, after all, really so much worse.

With my energy spent, my legs tired, and my bottom too sore to bike any further, I flagged down the chase car and bailed out on the day's ride. Back at the Golden Stage Inn, I found the father of the father-son trio, sitting alone in the living room with a bandaged knee and a bowl of pretzels, watching a World Series playoff game on TV. The man had fallen off his bicycle earlier in the day, had the wind knocked out of him and earned a few nasty scrapes, and had been forbidden by his sons from riding any more that weekend. I joined him with a couple of beers and was surprised to find, after watching the Yankees demolish Detroit, that, most miraculously, my mood had lifted after all.

Eventually, of course, the anger and the sadness and all the other assorted miseries of the divorce did go away. But nothing made that happen other than the simple passage of time. Of all the silly, tired old slogans, the only one I did hold on to was: *This Too Shall Pass.*

And it did.

Brave New Divorce

"We're going to do this divorce like it's never been done before," said my friend Ann.

Ann's husband had recently moved out of their house in Connecticut to an apartment in New York City. He had gone to Manhattan, of course, that void where all the divorced husbands go and subsequently disappear, leaving suburbia's divorcées to dateless and prospectless oblivion. But here was Ann, packing vegetables into containers for their two-week camping trip in an RV to Yosemite and a tour of the Rockies. They were all going together: Ann, her soon-to-be ex-husband, and their six- and eight-year-old sons. The separation papers would be awaiting them upon their return. But for the sake of the children, to keep things as normal as possible, even with a divorce on the horizon, the two parents would vacation with their children.

"We've been planning the trip a long time, and neither one of us wanted to miss out on it," said Ann. "And anyway, the fact that we're getting divorced doesn't mean we can't be friends . . . and good parents," she added.

It's not that I hadn't heard this kind of thing before. And it was something I had been thinking and wondering about quite a lot in the years following my divorce. But it was now six years after my own divorce, and I still didn't get this notion of "amicable divorce." Even—and here was the great surprise—as I found myself living it.

Amicable divorce. It seemed a contradiction in terms, an oxymoron. If things were amicable, why would we be getting a divorce?

Growing up, I was no stranger to divorce. My parents' marriage ended when I was six, in the late 1950s when divorce was still mentioned in a hush with downcast eyes. I later lived in the shadow of *The Brady Bunch* on TV—that sweet, bland, blended family in which the former spouses had conveniently disappeared, never threatening to cross the threshold of the Brady's peaceful home. That newly blended family was untouched by allegiances or discord, and certainly never the word *divorce*. (Although the Brady parents were tacitly understood to be widowed, there was never an unpleasant reference to death or grieving.) The blonde Brady girls, dressed in neat sixties turtlenecks and plaid jumpers, perched on perfectly made beds in clutterless rooms and chatted amiably with neat-combed, dark haired Brady boys. The stepsiblings plotted ventures like an anniversary surprise for their newlywed parents or conspired to track down a lost turtle. The kitchen table, overseen by the chipper, full-time live-in housekeeper Alice, was always empty, gleaming, and polished. No piles of schoolwork, no snack wrappers, no grocery circulars or PTA notices or stacks of bills. A clean, orderly wonderland of good cheer and pleasantness.

Looking back, I wonder: was it an insult, or a relief, to watch *The Brady Bunch,* mesmerized, from the crowded living room of my own not-so-amicably blended family? When my divorced mother married a man with four children of his own and moved them into our own small apartment where I lived with my two brothers, the results were anything but pleasant. There were conflicts, territorial battles. Toys destroyed, property trod on. Whispered alliances, hurt feelings, tears. Piles of mess everywhere—on the kitchen counters, on dressers, and under beds that became ad hoc storage areas for out-of-season clothes and school books and childhood treasures that no longer fit in closets or bookshelves. Hiding places were at a premium. The Brady's peaceable every-Tuesday-night-at-eight-o'clock home was laughable but compelling nevertheless. *If only,* I would think, with my brothers and stepsiblings crowded around the living room TV, slapping it occasionally to get the horizontal hold to stay in place, while watching placid Marsha Brady comb her long, silky hair.

But even more than that, from my childhood vantage point, the state of divorce between former spouses seemed inevitably drenched in both rancor and shame. My father had left my mother, with three children ages nine, six, and three, after falling passionately in love with another married woman in the neighborhood, a mother with three children of her own. In 1950s parlance, the two of them "ran off together," each leaving behind a betrayed spouse and three young children. With our father now living a three-hour drive away in another state, my two brothers and I saw him only during court-appointed visitations every third Saturday when he took the train to Penn Station, then a taxi to our apartment building. The fact that he would never even enter our building lobby, let alone the apartment upstairs, was understood. Instead, my brothers and I would wait for him at the curb, sometimes as long as an hour or more, until our father would appear in a taxi to whisk us down to Chinatown or the Statue of Liberty. Sometimes we would head for a midtown movie that was most likely already underway. (To fit the day into my father's train schedule, we missed the beginnings or endings of a great many movies.) The Saturday visits were mostly charac-terized by squabbles or whines over what toy or souvenir one of us coveted for that particular visit. Later the same day, my father would hail two yellow cabs at a time: one for the silent ride back uptown for my brothers and me, and the second for himself, heading downtown to Penn Station. I could imagine my father breathing a deep sigh of relief as he settled into his seat on the 4:41 to 30th Street Station, Philadelphia, then to his home where his new wife waited for him with a cold gin and tonic and a sympathetic ear.

That bad woman, according to my mother. That immoral home wrecker. What kind of a mother would leave her own children, after all? They were reprehensi-ble, both of them. His child support was a joke, a pittance. Judges were always on the father's side. Rare phone discussions were clipped, ending in a slammed receiver.

My mother and father hated each other, that much was clear. As I grew to adolescence and beyond, my mother felt freer to confide in me about my father's disloyalty, his underhandedness, and the damage he had wrought by his torrid affair. These confidences always seemed to escalate when there were money worries or when her attempts at new relationships came to their own, dismal ends. My father, on the other hand, barely acknowledged my mother's existence. He always steered the conversation to other innocuous areas.

Amicable divorce? What was that, anyway?

For a long time after my own divorce, I found the notions that ex-spouses must hate each other and the postdivorce life must be hell for all involved, hard lessons to unlearn. It was difficult, at first, not to be shocked as I watched my friends co-parenting amiably with divorced spouses. Even more amazing was witnessing how Bill and I found ourselves raising our children in this brave, new world of peaceful divorce. Bill attended every teacher conference, every band concert, every class play. Unthinkable. After our divorce, when I relocated with the children to a town in another state—but well within our agreed-upon fifty-mile radius—Bill, although annoyed at the inconvenience, followed suit to be closer to the children. Shocking. My children had friends, even sleepovers, at Bill's house. My own father could not have told me the name of my best friend or any of my teachers. He didn't know what day Girl Scouts met or that my creative dance teacher said I had rare talent. He knew nothing of where I spent my after-school afternoons or, for that matter, how I spent any day that wasn't visitation Saturday.

So here I was, a bit mystified, even as I fed school notices into the fax machine to Bill's office. *Robert's jazz band concert is May 18, Alex has a Little League game this Thursday at five. Remember to bring Robert to his orthodontist appointment next Saturday, your weekend, and when you're there, please speak to the doctor about the loose bracket on Robert's right molar.*

Unthinkable.

Knowing that this was the healthier, saner way of raising children of divorce, I sometimes found myself troubled and wondered why. Did it feel wrong for the simple reason that this was not how I was raised? When Bill came to the door of our home to pick up our sons for his regular Tuesday overnights, Wednesday dinners, and alternate weekends, he, like my father, was not invited in, but would wait in the driveway. The boys would fly out the door, and inevitably, I would run after them, with a jacket, notebook, notice, or forgotten school project they wanted to show their father. I would motion to him to roll down his window. "Did you bring back Alex's mitt from last weekend's Little League game?"

At times I would return to my empty house and find myself pondering. There was something unsettling about the notion that postdivorce life could be peaceable, even as I found myself reaping the benefits of it. What hurt the most was realizing how wasteful, how unnecessary it was, to have grown up with all that bitterness and rancor.

What if my father had known the name of my favorite teacher? What if my mother had let him in the door? What if he had, just once in all those lonely, yearning years, tucked me into bed? What if? What if?

And there was something even more, besides. Something in me did not want to be my ex-husband's friend. And why not? Certainly, during our marriage there was a basic foundation of friendship, even beneath all those years of strife. Bill and I could still, after a miserable fight, wake up on a Saturday morning to scrape peeling paint off the side of the house or pull weeds side by side. And even today, so many years and a million emotional miles apart, we share the same primary passion: the well-being of our children. There is no one with whom I trust my children as much as their father. There is no one else with whom I share the same pride when a son wins an award or looks breathtakingly handsome in a white shirt and suit, hair combed neatly. Bill and I beam over at each other, even as we hate each other.

Or do we?

Because if we don't hate each other, there comes the terrible question. If we don't hate each other—if we can be friendly, amicable, peaceful co-parents—then why are we divorced? Have we only perpetuated a life of more unnecessary pain? Different, but just as wasteful, just as wrong?

When Bill pulled into my driveway to drop off Alex after his baseball practice that week of Ann's RV vacation with her soon-to-be ex, I came to the door of his car. "Come look at what I did in my kitchen," I said to him. Wary, he slowly stepped out of the car and crossed the threshold into my house. "Look," I said, gesturing into the kitchen where he had never stood, only glimpsed from the doorway, "I ripped out that counter, and put in this round table instead. Big improvement, right?"

Stunned, Bill stepped into my kitchen and nodded. He didn't know what to say or what to think. Neither, at that moment, did I.

Trashing Dad

There was no shortage of how-to divorce books to instruct me how to remain sane and mature while going about the divorce process. The books spoke in calm, even tones about how to get divorced with dignity, how to be constructive and never destructive. How with the right attitude, the children would be just fine and I would emerge even better than before.

I had no patience for any of these books. I was too pissed. They only made me feel worse about the vindictive, angry person I feared my divorce was turning me into.

There was also no shortage of divorce memoirs—angry confessionals in which unhappy ex-wives spilled out accusations and tirades in self-righteous indignation. These only made me feel more frightened by reminding me just how bad my divorce still might become. I felt no comfort whatsoever that the women whose children were abducted by fathers to the Middle East or the ones left penniless after the ex-husband and new wife moved to Park Avenue had it even worse than I did. In my emotionally bruised state, other people's tragic divorces brought me no sense of kinship, but depressed me all the more.

Believe it or not, there was one book that did teach me a thing or two. Browsing the $2 remainder table in a seaside book store, I happened upon a book written by Ivana Trump with the promising title *The Best Is Yet to Come*. This, I figured, I could handle—probably escapist reading about how a woman had managed to make do after divorce with a mere $117 million plus the Plaza Hotel. But it turned out that Ivana, for all her society page hoopla, had been brought up in a fairly solid, middle class European family where hard work, discipline, and responsibility were highly prized. Her book had more to say than the expected "Don't get mad, get everything!" It also had some surprisingly sound, commonsense advice, like her most unexpected assertion that she would never speak ill of "The Donald" to her children. I found it amazing that this woman, publicly dumped after her husband's very public front-page-tabloid philandering with a ski bunny, could turn such a magnanimous cheek. She was aware of how damaging it would be to the children to hear their father trashed by her, the person whom they most relied upon and trusted—no matter what the rest of the world thought of him. She had somehow managed to put her children's best interests before her own and keep her feelings about him to herself.

This gave me pause, as I thought back to my feelings about my own father who had moved out when I was six. Until then, I had been something of a "daddy's girl," frequently photographed with my head of curls (like his), clinging to him as he walked me far, far into the ocean on summer trips to the beach. But in the years after my parents' divorce, my father was clearly earmarked as the transgressor in our lives—the enemy. "He left us," my mother reminded me with anger, over the years. Our broken home was all his fault. After all, hadn't it been his shameful behavior with that bad woman—I learned never to use the word *stepmother,* only the phrase *my father's wife*—that was the source of my mother's sad life and all of our financial woes? If I still loved that man with the warm brown skin who had carried me into the ocean, I tried not to think of it. Wouldn't it have been terribly disloyal to my mother, after all, to allow a glimmer of affection for this man who had broken her heart?

Several months after my father moved out, as we were pulling on our coats before one of his Saturday visits, my mother took my brothers and me aside. "I think you should stop calling him 'Daddy' now that he's left us," she said. "Call him 'Father' instead." We complied and never again called him "Daddy." However, neither my brothers nor I seemed to be comfortable calling him by the stilted "Father" to his face—so we no longer addressed him by any name at all. Among ourselves, we obediently referred to him as "Father." I can only imagine that my mother believed that orchestrating estrangement from his children, in whatever limited way she could, would be her only way to punish the man who had betrayed her.

The effect this had on my father, I never knew. But the sad irony was that, in her desire to punish my father, my mother had instead punished me. I was the girl without a daddy.

With the exception of the every-third-Saturday visitation, an annual, weeklong visit to his summer beach house in New Jersey, and, when I was older, the occasional restaurant dinner when he was in town on business, or weekend with him and his wife in Philadelphia, my father was not a part of my life. During my day-to-day life, full of schoolwork, friends, part-time jobs, and the social dramas of childhood and adolescence, I rarely thought about him. When I became a teenager, I ignored the clipped newspaper articles he occasionally sent me on some social or political issue we had disagreed on during our last lunch together. I couldn't have explained why I kept for so many years the gift he had given me for my tenth birthday—a small porcelain Cinderella statue that turned on a pedestal to tinkle out "So This Is Love," long after it had stopped working and long after the matching Cinderella watch was lost. Nor could I understand the sick hollowness filling my insides as I stepped on the train on Sunday nights from Philadelphia to New York's Penn Station after a weekend visit with my father. The candy bars I carried in my pockets for the ride home provided only the briefest distraction and did little to fill the emptiness.

Not long after my second son was born, my father was diagnosed with terminal lymphoma. It was incurable, although with treatment, he calmly told me over the phone, he might be able to live a long time with it. Only then, when I was overcome by a devastating and utterly inexplicable wave of pain, did I discover something so deeply hidden that it took my breath away. I discovered that I loved my father. I realized that I had always loved my father and I had spent much of my childhood yearning for him. Throughout the years, as I grew, I missed his Aqua Velva scent and the flip-flops he wore to the beach during my once-a-year summer visit.

And I realized something more. Every choice I had made, my college major, my job choices, had been motivated by a hidden desire to please him—maybe even to get him to love me back. To make him sorry that he had left me when he had left my mother so many years before.

I had stumbled upon these startling truths *almost* too late. But fortunately, there was still time. In the three years in which one chemotherapy treatment after another failed to arrest the cancer's progression, I made frequent trips to my father's home in Philadelphia. There we were finally able to talk with the depth of feeling and affection that had for so long been bottled up on both sides. He was able to express to me, if not in so many words then certainly in feeling, the extent of his loss of his children's presence in his life all those years ago. He had wanted to know more of our lives but had been shut out. I realized that my father had been powerless to do anything but resign himself to the effect of my mother's portrayal of him. And on the day of my last visit, I knew by the way his eyes lit up when I entered his dim study with a pastrami sandwich, and by how hard he tried to eat it for my benefit, how much he loved me. In those final, waning weeks of his life, we were finally able to tell each other "I love you." When he died at age sixty-one, my loss was magnified by deep, searing regret for what had been the greater loss all those years.

I thought often of this after Bill and I divorced. With my young sons in mind, I recalled how both of my brothers, despite blazing intelligence, had struggled with self-esteem issues as they grew older. I wondered how different their lives might have been and how much more confidence they might have had to meet life's challenges had they had a man in their lives who was truly interested in them—who attended their Little League games and clarinet concerts, and who let them know he believed in them.

Reflecting on this, once again I realized that my legacy as the child of a badly managed divorce turned out to be more valuable to me than any how-to-get-divorced book. I firmly decided that regardless of how I ever felt about Bill, I would not do the same to my children. He would always be their father and a major part of those three boys. What would I be saying about them were I to malign him? I realized that giving my sons permission to love their father, and to receive his love for them, would be perhaps my greatest gift to them.

But it wasn't going to be easy. I would have to keep my occasional anger or bitterness from these three people to whom I was closest in the world, both in proximity and emotion. I knew that my children could read my mood by my expression or by the way I set their plates before them. I would have to monitor myself carefully, so that no complaining phone calls to friends occurred when they were in earshot. Even worse, I would constantly have to conjure up Bill's presence when he was the last thing I wanted to think about. "Did you show Dad?" I would ask when they brought home a graded assignment or a mention in the school newspaper. "Make sure Dad sees the 'A' you got on your algebra test; don't forget, you wanted to get him to help with your science project." I forwarded to Bill every notice of a Boy Scout meeting, every announcement of a new father-son program offered by the Y, every parent observation evening. Not only did I make it possible for their father to be in my sons' lives, I encouraged it in every way possible.

It felt like it all backfired when Bill, who himself worked hard to maintain a close, involved relationship with our sons, moved to the new town where I had deliberately relocated after the marriage. *No good deed goes unpunished,* I thought, with not a little irony, recalling my relief in moving to a town where I might never run into him. But now here he was, ambling from classroom to classroom at every Open School Night, seated across the auditorium before every school orchestra and band concert, regularly pulling up in our driveway, in his assistant Scoutmaster cap, to pick up Alex for a Boy Scout meeting.

I sometimes wondered whether Bill would give me—give our children—the same consideration of never speaking ill of me. I couldn't be sure. Certainly he had a great many grievances against me. He left the marriage feeling angry and betrayed. There were things he might have done to try to make the boys no longer love me—chief among them, to portray me as the cause of the divorce and destruction of their former lives. But there was nothing I could do to affect or control that. I couldn't undo the past. In the end I believe that out of love for our sons, Bill reached the same conclusion I did. Because love me they did.

Today, my sons have fiercely close and loyal relationships with both of their parents. I believe it is the foundation of their lives and gives them the confidence to take risks in life and stretch beyond their limits. Their parents' steadfast presence in their lives and our love for them are certainties. This knowledge has settled deep inside them. My hope is that it will stay with them though all the hard times that surely lay ahead, and long after we are gone.

Divorce in the Age of E-mail

once held the misguided notion that the main benefit of divorce would be not having to interact daily with a person with whom I no longer got along. Wasn't that the point, after all? No longer to have in my life that person who had become an adversary and an irritant? And how wonderful it would be no longer to have to run decisions by him. No longer to be subject to his disapproval of everything from my occasional "Oh, shit!" in front of the children, to my New Yorker slang ("sounds low class," he would say). I'll admit he may have been somewhat justified to be annoyed by my chronic inability to leave the house when I said I'd be ready ("Why can't I ever get you out of the house on time?" he would say with frustration, coat on, car running, while I ran upstairs to grab or check on just one more thing, or give yet another final instruction to the babysitter). But what a relief it would be no longer to live with a man who, from my point of view, had some kind of unhealthy fixation on being on time for absolutely everything. "This isn't the army," I would argue. Couldn't he cut me a little slack?

Well, that's over, I told myself, relieved. Or so I thought.

What happened instead was that once formally separated and with three children shuttling between us, Bill and I found ourselves having to interact not less but far more than we had before. Myriad issues that had been handled independently by either one of us now became the subject of constant back and forth. I'd dial his office: the fifth grade orchestra concert was a week from Tuesday at seven; did he get the notice? He would leave a voice mail: the boys are out of pajamas at his house, please send some over. Another call to him: had he sent me that reimbursement check for religious school?

And the scheduling issues! "Could I switch this Friday night for next week," he would ask me, "I have unexpected plans." "I'll be getting back from my weekend away late," I would tell him. "Would you please bring the boys back on Sunday after dinner rather than before?" Fortunately, each of us seemed to have figured out that it paid to be agreeable to these requests whenever possible because the flexibility would work both ways. I can never figure out why certain divorced parents I know, women and men both, insist on making a point of denying any request for a schedule change—perhaps out of a sense of vindication or spite.

I tried to keep the phone calls as even-toned and emotionally detached as possible. But it was hard. This was, after all, the man I had been married to for nineteen

years. I could detect the tiniest hint of impatience or derision in his voice, even on an answering machine—a
peaceful afternoon could become nearly ruined before
one of his messages was even fully replayed. Old resent-
ments would resurface at the most innocuous comment.
And of course, he still had that fixation with being on
time. "I'll be here to pick them up Friday at five o'clock.
Please have them ready so I'm not left waiting in the
driveway like last time." Instantly my defenses would
spring to attention. "They're not soldiers, they're little
boys," I would shoot back. "This isn't the military!" And
there we were, sparring again just like in the old days.

What was the point of being divorced? I sometimes wondered, guilty and exasperated, as the boys, twelve minutes past the sacred five o'clock deadline, finally drove
off in Bill's car. And how could we both—okay, I'll speak
for myself—how could I manage to become so juvenile
as to find myself once again squabbling like a hostile sib-
ling? Looking at myself that way wasn't entirely comfortable. At times I did have to question whether I might
be replaying childhood conflicts with my older brother,
a habit formed long before my marriage. Add to this all
the new grievances against Bill I had gathered during the
divorce process itself, and I was ready within a thirty second conversation to combust like corn dust in a silo.

Then we discovered the most wonderful invention,
even better than answering machines: e-mail.

In the world of the divorced parent, e-mail was about
the best thing to come along since the notion of joint
custody. Now we could package any arrangement,
request, or schedule change in an impersonal digital

message. No tone of voice, no blaming innuendo. Just a simple "Would you be willing to switch Tuesday for Wednesday?" and the task would be accomplished. Weeks, even months would go by when I never needed to hear his voice, nor he mine. It had a remarkably positive impact on my psyche. Now my life was filled only with the affectionate, respectful, or loving voices of the people I chose to have in my life.

However, the downside of e-mail, as I soon discovered, was that it was all too easy to shoot off a message in an angry mood, which I will guiltily admit to doing from time to time. As a writer, at times I could not resist the opportunity to wax eloquent with my grievances. "If you can afford to take them skiing, which you well know I cannot, then you should be able to pay for ski clothes, including those gloves I buy them that they keep losing when they're with you. And while we're on the subject of lost items . . . "

On the other hand, e-mails could be easily deleted without being read, and I began to suspect Bill of doing exactly that. Although this thought annoyed me immensely (all that hard work composing scathing epistles for nothing!), it was probably the best thing in the long run for all concerned. Somehow, what needed to be scheduled or arranged always was.

Then there was the common problem of a child's school report accidentally left on the other parent's computer but due tomorrow. This, too, was hugely alleviated when we began to use laptops and the Internet. Each boy could now carry his entire school and social life back and forth with him. No more reports or school newspaper articles left on Dad's computer. No more need to run home to check the computer for an e-mail from the teacher with the next day's assignment.

Unfortunately, e-mail could do little to solve the other perpetual problem of forgetting at the other parent's house something that was absolutely, positively needed for school the next day. I would admonish the boys that it was their responsibility, not mine, to keep track of their things and to plan for what they needed where and when. At the same time I knew that admonishments would be far less effective than consequences—simply allowing them to show up at school without the forgotten item. But with divorced parental guilt always ready to rear its ugly head at a moment's notice, this was excruciatingly difficult to enforce. The old demon voice would hiss in my ear: *Isn't it my fault, after all, that the children have to shuttle between two houses?* As a result Bill and I were constantly hightailing it to each other's homes with forgotten items.

As the years went on, even this got easier. The once-dreaded teenage driver's license became a godsend. Soon after David passed his driving test and received the coveted prize, he bought himself a used car with the last of his Bar Mitzvah money and the proceeds of three years busing tables in a local restaurant. Car proud, and as the first son to achieve this exalted privilege, David readily agreed to any request for a run to the drugstore or to his Dad's house. Whether this was due to his teenage zeal for any opportunity to get behind the wheel or simply David's remarkable good nature, I didn't know. But I was grateful just the same. Two years later Robert was driving as well, and I was home free. Any worry I had about my sons' driving safety was alleviated when I realized that they, with youthful reflexes and many months of Drivers Ed behind them, were safer and more capable drivers than I, a New Yorker who hadn't learned to drive until I was in my twenties. On family trips, I even happily let David or Robert take the wheel. When someone invariably "Shotgunned!" the front seat, I was all too glad to snooze in the back.

So technology and teenage drivers' licenses had made my life infinitely easier. But now I had another problem. As they matured, all three of my sons, even the youngest, developed a fierce—what I would call unhealthy—fixation on being on time. And there I was, once again the object of someone's impatience at my failure to hand them their breakfast or lunch money or permission slips in time to enable them to shoot out the door at precisely 7:05 each morning. Heading out together for some family event, they would fret at my inability to leave the house when I said I would be ready. Bill had had his revenge. I now had three little Bill surrogates to be impatient with me.

One Sunday night not long ago, I promised to take the four of us to a favorite local seafood restaurant. It was an unusual splurge but felt like a nice way to end a relaxing weekend together. I asked David to phone ahead for a six o'clock reservation. "Remember, Mom, we have to leave here by no later than quarter of six," David repeatedly told me that afternoon. And again. "Mom, we have to leave the house in an hour. . . . Mom, we're leaving in a half hour. You'll be ready, right?"

I did my best. But this was, after all, Sunday. After a lot of last-minute dashing around, I finally climbed into the car at about two minutes before six. Since the three of them had been waiting in the car for me, I withheld the impulse to remind them that this wasn't the military, after all, and stayed guiltily silent.

When we walked into the Mansion Clam House at quarter after six, David turned to me with a triumphant smile. "We're exactly on time," he said. "I really made the reservation for six fifteen, but I told you six o'clock. I know you, Mom."

I was awestruck at the simplicity of it. Now that was love. Which, in the end, means a whole lot more to me than technology any day.

Eating and Drinking

I ate my way through my divorce. There is no other way to say it.

I had been an up-and-down dieter most of my life. Rarely, if ever, the weight I wanted to be, I usually hovered between five and twenty pounds over my ideal weight. Although no one would ever have called me overweight, I had always been intensely concerned about the shape of my body since the day that my mother exclaimed, seeing my thirteen-year-old potbelly, "Jessica, we have to put you on a diet!" But I probably wasn't any more obsessed than most other teenagers who devoured *Seventeen* and *Glamour,* and who at one time believed that looking fabulous in a pair of Calvins was one of the highest accomplishments a girl could achieve.

As I grew older, and particularly during my marriage, my tendency to gain weight was usually linked to my mood. I gained weight when I was bored or depressed, then successfully dieted it off when I was either in love, pumped up about a new job, or motivated by the new season's shorter skirts. This hardly seemed unusual, since it was a routine to which a good many of my friends also admitted. Fortunately, I was a highly disciplined, gung ho dieter. Over the years I gamely tried almost every weight loss program that celebrities or friends swore by, joined gyms regularly, and was fairly diligent about burning off calories—my one and only motivation for exercising— by putting in time on some aerobic machine or in a swimming pool several times a week.

Still, I was a classic yo-yo. After a period of blown diets, there was always a certain number, about twenty pounds over my "goal," when the mental alarm bells would sound and launch me resolutely into the next diet-and-exercise phase. Before long I was back to being tantalizingly close to my goal weight by five to seven pounds. I could live with that. If I didn't fit my size sixes, I didn't look too bad in my size eights. (Of course my closet contained a range of sizes.) I once even reached my Weight Watchers goal weight—for about five minutes—before rewarding myself with a celebratory trip to Ben & Jerry's.

Eating to cheer myself up, dull some pain, distract myself from distress, or simply pass the time seemed perfectly normal. Better yet, unlike most methods of emotionally "checking out," it was entirely legal. Food was an entirely innocent substance, was it not? Certainly gaining weight held none of the stigma of alcoholism or drug addiction.

Because a good portion of my married years was spent in that vague, depressed state that something was not quite right—what was not right, of course, was living in constant conflict with my husband—comfort foods, usually sweets or breads, comprised a large part of my life. One Halloween night, after a particularly awful fight with Bill, I retreated to the patio behind my house with a bag of miniature Milky Way bars and discovered how difficult it was to cry and to eat candy at the same time. This did not, however, stop me from putting away a good many Milky Ways.

Then my marriage fell apart, and my habit of dulling my feelings with food developed into a full-blown eating disorder.

Plunging into the new full-time job of getting divorced, my days were filled with painful end-of-marriage discussions with Bill, conferences with my lawyer, mounting legal bills, and attempts to manage finances, find an affordable new house, and then pack up my large house to move myself and the children.

Throughout all this, my evenings were filled with food. Nightly I tried to escape the fear, anger, and anxiety with comfort-laden foods. It wasn't just food—it was wine, too. Anything that helped me "zone out" for a little while was welcome. If a few glasses of wine and a bag of Doritos couldn't make me completely forget that my world was falling apart, at least it was a serviceable distraction. A late afternoon glass of white wine—made somehow more acceptable and less calorie-laden by the addition of club soda and lots of ice—quickly followed by another became habit. Busy with the children in the evenings, my own dinners were usually on-the-run grazing for which an afternoon of snacking left me little appetite but didn't stop me from eating nonetheless.

While a glass or two of wine did offer significant temporary relief from stress, I never crossed the line into what one would call serious drinking. This was partially due to the fact that more than two drinks or glasses of wine would make me uncomfortably woozy and, in fairly short order, ill. But the real reason that my divorce didn't turn me into a full-blown alcoholic was that my true "substance of choice" was not alcohol, but food. A glass or two of Cabernet or a salt-encrusted, frosty margarita were really only the "border drugs" that powered up my appetite and propelled me into eating. Something sweet or carbohydrate-laden could do as much to lift my spirits or calm me down as any mind-altering drug. Briefly. Foods that harkened back to moments in my grandmother's kitchen, like fresh rye bread, rice pudding, or chewy chocolate chip cookies, had a particular power to soothe me.

When I hung up after an angry phone conversation with Bill, I would grab a bag of tortilla chips. With an utterly ridiculous "I'll show him!" attitude, I would feel entitled to eat the whole bag—as though by doing so I was punishing Bill and not me (thus, the logic of a true addict). When the boys had their milk and cookies at bedtime, so did I. I deserved it with all that was going on, didn't I? Nights had their own terrors. Sleeping alone for the first time in decades, the fears would emerge. Some sweet, soft, carbohydrate-rich "snack"—a sleeve of Chips Ahoy, the leftover Italian bread—would regularly accompany me to my bedroom at night. In this way, temporarily, I would not be alone.

With the next morning came guilt and remorse. *Why on earth did I eat that yesterday?* became my first thought of each day. Of course I was putting on weight, although not as quickly as I might have, since I was now working overtime to offset the eating with punishing spin classes and longer stints on the StairMaster.

None of these behaviors made any sense. They are also, as I later learned, the hallmarks of addiction. I was truly out of control. Stepping on the scale one morning, I was shocked to discover that I had exceeded my alarm-bells number. Then, I hit five pounds over that number. Then ten pounds over. Soon I was inching toward fifteen. The sirens kept sounding, and I heard them loud and clear. But I kept eating.

Never one to give up on the idea of redemption, I began and then quickly failed one new diet program after another. A $100-an-hour nutritionist told me I should just start eating three good meals a day and gave me a list of snacks and other foods on which I was instructed to go "cold turkey." *Tell me something I don't know,* I thought. By the next day, I had opened and finished an entire box of pretzels—"Baldies," they were called—that had been a particular favorite of my grandfather's when I was a little girl. The following week, the nutritionist gently suggested that perhaps this wasn't the best time for me to attempt to lose weight. Maybe I needed all those comfort foods while I was going through my divorce.

It was a tempting proposition. But much as I loved the idea of having carte blanche to comfort myself with unlimited food, I knew that obesity, a condition I simply could not bear, would be the result. The idea of a better future for myself after the divorce was quickly fading. I could never hope to have another relationship, certainly never start dating. I would be fat. Who would want me?

But something else was terribly wrong. I recognized that what I had done, in these months of reaching for food as a buffer against the highly uncomfortable feelings brought on by the divorce, was to compound my already problem-laden life with an even bigger problem. Now, along with facing divorce, financial insecurity, and guilt, I had also managed to seriously erode my own self-esteem—not only with an unattractive body but also with my lack of self-control. I knew enough to recognize that I had a serious problem. And this wasn't a simple little dieting problem any more. Legal though it might be, I was as hooked on eating to escape reality as the most down-and-dirty crack addict. By now, my life was increasingly burdened less by divorce than by the emotional wreckage caused by uncontrolled eating.

Eventually it wasn't even the weight I was putting on that bothered me so much. It was the behavior. There was something utterly degrading about being so out of control—me, who had gotten straight As throughout school, two degrees at an Ivy League school, and never stepped outside my house with a run in my stocking or a spot on a blouse. Me, whose standards were sky-high in almost everything else in life. How could I be reduced to having so little control! At my most downcast, I didn't even care how I looked. What I couldn't abide was witnessing my own inability to stop eating. It became excruciating. Unbearable.

It was this desperation that saved me.

Months and then a year went by. We had made progress on the divorce. Our Custodial and Residential Access Agreement had been negotiated and signed, the marital home had been sold, and I had purchased our new home that, while cozy and promising, was in need of many repairs before we could move in. The boys and I were living in a rental house in our old town while they finished the school year. After putting them on the school bus each morning, I made a forty-five-minute drive to the new house, where I checked on the progress of various carpenters, painters, and other workmen. I could not yet imagine our new life in this town where we would be complete strangers.

Late one Tuesday evening—the night the children regularly stayed over with Bill—I sat alone in the kitchen of the new house. The room was a mess—a rainstorm had revealed numerous leaks in the window over the sink and flooded the windowsill. The painters had begun scraping, and the countertops and floor were covered with paint chips and dust. On the counter was a box of bakery breakfast pastries—cheese and cinnamon Danish, crullers, one or two glazed donuts—that had been sent over earlier that day as a welcome gift by my new neighbor across the street. By now the pastries were cold and clammy, as such things get late in the day when they have sat around since morning. They were also my dinner. Although I was growing increasingly nauseated, I kept picking away at them, piece by piece. I could barely taste their sweetness, but it didn't matter. I kept trying for that blissful moment of calm, that flood of well-being that, no matter how brief, normally came with the first bite. But this time, it never came. All I felt was desolate. I opened the box once more and considered trying again. For a few long moments, I looked at the sugar icing on the remaining pastries. Then I closed the box.

Aside from the paint scrapings, the almost finished box of pastries, and the user's manual that had come with the new stove, there was only one other item in the kitchen: a telephone directory. I looked up a 12-step program for food addicts modeled on Alcoholics Anonymous. There it was, with an 800 number.

Some years before, when searching for the next diet program, I had dropped in on a few meetings but had not returned. *Those people are really bad,* I thought. *They call themselves addicts.* And they talked a lot about a "Power Greater Than Ourselves," which seemed completely unrelated to my weight problem. If there was a God, I was fairly certain that the last thing He would care about was whether I had broken another diet. Besides, their "spiritual" solution was filled with a lot of generalities that didn't help me figure out how to lose weight, which is all I had come for. In any case, these people said that they were powerless over food. *That isn't me,* I thought. *I can always diet, once I get around to it. This isn't where I belong.*

But now it was.

My desperation had given me a new willingness to be open to any solution. But even more than that, my divorce had changed me. If I had learned anything by the complete overturning of the so-called secure married life to which I once clung, it was that my sheer willpower was not enough to order the universe exactly the way I wanted it to be. The illusion that I could maintain a good marriage and a perfect home life for my children, not to mention a perfect size six, by relying on all those qualities I so prized in myself—intelligence, superior education, self-discipline—had been shattered. For the first time, perhaps, I was willing to admit that my way of doing things was not necessarily the best way. This led to a painful and frightening proposition: if I was as incapable of taking charge of my life as I was of controlling my eating—which I so clearly had proven—wouldn't chaos and helplessness be the result?

Facing this would take tremendous courage. But I had already discovered something else about myself that I had not known before the divorce. I made the miraculous discovery that I possessed far more courage than I once thought. It was my lack of courage that had kept me trapped in my marriage for many unhappy years. But by handling my end of the divorce process, then finding a new home and building a new life for myself and my children, I had grown. I had enlarged my store of courage as one develops a muscle—by sheer use. I decided I was now ready to take on another challenge I had once believed insurmountable: my addiction to food.

The following Saturday I was sitting at a table with about thirty cheerful, bright-eyed people, mostly women but also a few men, on the second floor of a nearby church. By some odd stroke of luck—or perhaps it really was that Power Greater Than Ourselves that they kept referring to in the meeting—my new house turned out to be located less than a mile from a church that held one of the largest collections of 12-step meetings in the county.

At first I was certain I had walked into the wrong room—these people were mostly thin. And happy. Many were well dressed, clearly professional, and well educated. *How odd,* I thought. This was not the group of addicts I had expected to find in this church.

The meeting began, and I discovered something even more curious. Not only were these slender, attractive people not sitting around bemoaning their status as "compulsive overeaters," they cheerfully admitted it, while professing only gratitude for their recovery from their food addiction. As a further stroke of luck, this particular meeting, while founded on the principles of AA, turned out to be a kind of 12-step subgroup that didn't just offer spiritual generalities but adhered to a clearly defined food plan. It consisted of three healthy meals of measured amounts of proscribed foods a day, with nothing in between. It also included no alcohol, no sugar, and none of my comfort foods. A smiling woman sitting next to me gave me her phone number and instructed me to call her at eight o'clock the next morning to tell her what items on the food plan I would eat that day. I now had a sponsor. "Try it for one day," she told me. "You can always change your mind." I learned that they did this one day at a time, just as in Alcoholics Anonymous.

It was terribly humbling and at first painfully embarrassing to admit that I could not stop my compulsive eating behavior without help. But apparently this place was, in one of the group's slogans, "the last house on the block." Their food plan turned out to be the magic formula for my body that started a steady weight loss. While it included many high-calorie protein foods that were strictly prohibited in every diet I had tried, it also eliminated the carbohydrates and sugars that inevitably lead to compulsive eating for me and others for whom those substances are highly addictive. Miraculously, the craving for carbohydrates and sweets quickly disappeared. But most important, the program offered a different kind of group support than any other weight-loss program I had ever encountered. Instead of talking about diet recipes, they talked about feelings, old wounds, and a search for spirituality. Desperate to put my life in order, I reached out for that support, continued to attend meetings, and from then on, as far as food was concerned, I did what I was told. "If you want what we have, you do what we do," they told me.

And so I did. It took just a few months for all the weight I had gained, and more, to fall off. Not only did I hit that magical goal number, but also went several pounds below it. Years later, I have not gained any of it back.

But I know now that keeping my eating under control is about so much more than my jeans size. Regaining a mastery over this formerly uncontrollable addiction propelled my self-esteem higher than any academic degree or professional achievement had ever taken me. When the time came to start a new career, begin dating, and embark on my new life, I sailed into my future with full confidence. I had to admit that I looked pretty good.

But to this day, I do not do it alone.

Kitchens I

ver since that day I stood in my white Mexican cotton wedding dress and thought, "Oh, hell . . . if it doesn't work out, I can always get a divorce," I have done a good amount of soul-searching about why I had been so foolhardy as to have married with this thought in mind. Aside from being far too young at twenty-two, I have never been able to come up with an exact explanation. But I always knew it had something to do with a red mixing spoon.

I was six years old when my parents' marriage came to a crashing end. It was the late 1950s, when divorce was regarded at best as outright failure, and at worst, shameful. Families with "broken homes" were rarely mentioned except in gossip—and of that, there was plenty. Ours had its particular veil of shame, since my parents' marriage ended in a scandal when my father fell in love with one of the other mothers in our close-knit neighborhood.

After my father and his new wife moved to another state—a three hours' drive away—my two brothers and I saw him only during court-appointed visitations.

My twenty-nine-year-old mother, distraught and heartbroken, had been left to raise three small children. With minimal alimony and child support, and neither job nor college degree—she had quit college at nineteen to marry my father—she had scant ability to provide for the four of us. But somehow she did.

One way she managed was to lean heavily for help on her one daughter. From the age of about seven, I immediately stepped into the role of caretaker and housekeeper for my mother and brothers. I willingly handled any chore—running downstairs to the basement laundry room of our portion of a rented two-family house, gingerly lighting the oven pilot light to make dinner, learning to carefully wipe delicate plant leaves and dust mop under chairs and the sofa. I was also my grieving mother's support and confidante—sympathizing with her troubles, keeping her company on shopping trips, and in my early teen years, helping her get ready for dates. I did not resent these adult duties and took them on willingly. In fact I derived an enormous sense of comfort and self-esteem from this exalted semiparent position.

When I was ten, my mother married again, which resulted in a move to New York City. It also meant teary good-byes to school friends and a beloved fourth grade teacher. That marriage also came with something that was to radically change life at home: three stepsisters and a stepbrother, close in age. These children, who had recently lost their own mother to cancer, quickly became part of my life. There was much chaos in the new blended household with crowded bedrooms and over-stuffed closets. But they were closets that soon became once again empty, since the marriage turned out even more disastrously than the first, and ended only four years later, leaving me to say good-bye to those children as well. Always one to easily attract men, and with per-petual optimism that the next marriage would finally be the right one, my mother was, throughout my teen years, sometimes involved in relationships that included the possibility of remarriage and more stepsiblings. (My mother found that good marriage, finally, at the age of forty-six, when I was already in graduate school. The marriage was to remain solid and peaceful for the next twenty years, until she became widowed. Then yet again, my mother happily remarried. But that's another story.)

In short, the home in which I grew up was a continu-ally disrupted and unsettled place.

Throughout all of that, teachers, aunts, and my mother's admiring friends often noted what a remark-ably well-adjusted child I was. The unspoken subtext, of course, was "considering the divorce." Unlike my broth-ers, who made a point of underachieving or getting into minor mishaps, I excelled in my schoolwork, staying at the top of almost every class from kindergarten through high school. I had lots of friends and idolized my teach-ers, who usually considered me among their favorites. School life was orderly, predictable, and pleasant. I dreaded the school day's end at quarter after three, when I would return to the strain and the chores of home.

Through it all I was, yes, the remarkably helpful and

well-adjusted child. But inside of me was a place I never revealed and scarcely could even name myself, although it was always there. It was as though some tender place inside me had enlarged to become a huge, raw well of anxiety. It was also a place of deep, searing loneliness. There were times, like on rainy days or afternoons after school when the apartment was empty, that the well felt so cavernous it seemed bigger than my own body. There was always the sense that the world was unsafe and insecure, ready to be overturned at any moment. Within that hollow place in my body, fears about what lay around the corner, in the mail, in the jangling of the black living room telephone, always lurked. After my mother's second divorce, with her alimony now gone and a new baby from the second marriage having arrived, the financial strain became even worse. My mother took a full-time job along with various part-time jobs in the evenings and on Saturdays. I was fourteen now and had become even more important to the household than before. For this, I was grateful.

My mission in life became keeping this unsteady world in order. Security at school meant maintaining perfect grades. At home I would keep life secure by maintaining a predictable and orderly domestic routine. This mostly involved grocery shopping, housekeeping, babysitting my younger siblings, and cooking for my brothers and baby sister while my mother worked. If there was dinner on the table at five thirty—not quarter after five, not quarter of five—if the smell of food filled the kitchen, then there would be, at least, a predictable end to the day.

My mother, a distracted and completely disinterested

cook, taught me to defrost frozen fish and sprinkle it with paprika, and open canned vegetables and heat them in a saucepan. Frozen French fries, the store-brand kind that no one really liked, were the usual "starch." Before each meal, I set the table carefully, and here, too, was order: napkin folded, fork on the left, knife and spoon on the right. When dinner was over I remained in the still-warm kitchen where I did homework and studied hard. Nearby my mother's dinner, covered with foil, waited to be rewarmed when she got home from her evening job.

When I left home and went to college, it felt that my life had finally begun. I lost myself in the joys of academic pursuit and, for the first time, social pleasures. Equally intoxicating was the dizzying sense of liberation that came from being responsible for no one other than myself. I reveled in my comfortable cocoon of college life. But as I neared senior year, the old anxiety returned. Fear of life in the world beyond college haunted me. And then, at age twenty and about to graduate from college and be cast into that uncertain world, I met Bill while buying a backpack in a bicycle and camping goods store.

Bill, it turned out, didn't just work in the store, he owned it. He was also about to start graduate school. Besides the small store, he had a used car he had paid for himself, two long-married parents, and no college loans. We had a few dates, and I came back after graduation for a visit. The visit lasted a weekend, a month, the next year. We went out for Italian dinners, and Bill always paid the check.

Time passed, and I toyed with the idea of graduate

school. But there seemed no reason to leave my comfortable college town life with Bill. Since we had been basically living together anyway, it didn't seem like a very momentous step to find a larger apartment together and put both of our names on the mailbox. Bill was calm and even-tempered; he could do comforting things like change a flat tire in a matter of minutes, or pull a tissue from his pocket, without my asking, when my nose ran. But there was another attraction, although I could not have explained it at the time. The apartment we found had a big, old-fashioned kitchen with a table in the middle and a fairly decent stove. Bill covered most of one kitchen wall with a large pegboard and painted it yellow. On it I hung kitchen tools I began collecting, one by one, like jewels. A corkscrew. A tomato knife and a wire whisk. A set of shiny, red melamine spoons, one plain, one slotted, and a spatula to match. A gleaming French cast-iron omelet pan that added a splash of bright blue. A strainer. A bread knife. As I filled the board's empty spaces, I could ignore, for that day or that moment, the empty space inside me that was always there, even in our new apartment. Somehow, each new item assuaged the fearful ache a little more—or at least, distracted me from it.

Bill was a vegetarian, which presented me with a new cooking challenge. At night while he studied for business school exams, I pored over and practically memorized *The Vegetarian Epicure* and the *Moosewood Cookbook*. I learned to cook millet soufflé and eggplant parmesan. We got a cat. This was home.

Almost two years later, we called our parents one Sunday morning to tell them that we had decided to get married. Something did not feel right, and I knew it. But once we had somehow agreed to it over dinner the night before, I felt paralyzed to back out of the decision or even to put my misgivings into words. *Is this true love?* I wondered. I wasn't sure. Things with Bill were not perfect. But I had a safe home now, and a reliable friend and partner. As Bill spoke to his parents, I looked down to find that I was cradling one red mixing spoon in my hand. By then I had a set of red melamine mixing bowls to match the red spoon. *Yes,* I thought. *This is too good to give up. This home, for better or worse, will not be broken.* I took the phone and agreed with Bill's parents that it would make sense to get married in late summer, after his graduation from business school and before the start of our new jobs in New York City.

Later that day, with the phone calls behind us and a long, empty afternoon stretching ahead, I baked bread. The feel of the dough in my hands, the smell of baking whole grain loaves, pushed down deep any sense of misgiving—or was it foreboding?—the morning's announcement had aroused.

Seven months later, we were married. As a wedding gift we received a set of French enamel pots to match the omelet pan.

After marriage we left our college town and moved to New York City. I loved the city; it was where I had grown up, and I knew the streets and the neighborhoods as home. For years, I had looked forward to the day I would take my place among the busy, bright people in crisp shirts and leather satchels rushing through the glass doors of important skyscrapers. My first job made good on that promise, as I had been awarded a New York City Urban Fellowship that landed me a position in the first deputy mayor's office, in a historic building alongside City Hall. I rushed to meetings in my tweed blazer and stood along the wall in the City Hall Blue Room where the mayor held televised press conferences. I buzzed myself into the corridor that led to the mayor's office, passing the fabled smoke-filled Room 9 where the journalists lounged after deadline. It felt as though the blood and adrenaline ran through my veins with the same intensity as the subway line that rumbled from our apartment near Union Square to the City Hall station. I was here. I was part of things. I had my place in the world.

And I was married. In our small Third Avenue apartment, my blue French enamel pots hung on the kitchen wall. Though my kitchen was so small that I could stand between the stove and refrigerator and touch opposite walls with my two hands, I loved every inch of it. There was no room for a pegboard, only a cramped Formica counter where my kitchen spoons, whisk, spatulas, and tongs now nestled in a blue and white ceramic canister. Through a small window over the sink, the distant twin towers of the World Trade Center reflected morning sun and at night glowed with a thousand tiny lit windows. I cooked lamb chops in a countertop broiler, chopped herbs and parsley on a small wooden board that hung on a leather cord from a brass hook screwed into the wall. I had my place in the world. Once again, I had my kitchen. When I was in my kitchen, either simultaneously managing four separate pots on our apartment sized four-burner stove, lining the metal shelves with shelf paper, or simply soaping and rinsing my serving spoons and spatulas, I felt at peace. Bill was more than content to leave the small space to me, while enjoying the complicated vegetarian dishes and other culinary marvels my kitchen produced. Life was good, except when he and I were having some strained conversation.

By that first year after our marriage, Bill and I were already in couple's therapy.

Bill hated living in the city. He desperately wanted to live somewhere rural, in a house rather than this tenth-story "box," as he called it, with neighbors who did no more than nod brusquely at you. He couldn't sleep at night with the constant boom from the street below when taxis landed after flying over a dip in the badly paved Third Avenue. Bill read gardening books and seed catalogues. He wanted a garden, he said, where he could plant tomatoes and green beans like his father did.

The idea of leaving the city depressed me. Even worse was the idea of commuting by diesel train, and then by subway, from some distant rural town to City Hall Station. The thought of the suburbs was to me, as it is to many born-and-bred New Yorkers, akin to a death sentence. But hoping that a happier husband would make for a better marriage, I gave in.

With the proceeds of the camping goods store that Bill sold when he graduated, we made a down payment on a four-room ranch house about an hour's train ride north of the city. It was on a little over an acre, crowded with overgrowth. Over the summer Bill hacked at the weeds to reveal the view of a sloping hillside and small pond below. Now we had our own kitchen walls where Bill secured a six-foot-long wooden plank; on it he installed S-hooks where my blue enamel pots, two saucepans, omelet pan, and frying pan to match, hung in a neat row. I attached a bouquet of dried thyme to the last hook at the end.

I hated the suburbs. I resented every minute of what turned out to be a two-hour commute each way on trains that frequently stalled or broke down. I met Bill at the train station each night exhausted and resentful. But on weekends, I did love my kitchen with the red and blue tattersall wallpaper. With morning sunlight streaming through the windows, the pattern perfectly set off the red spoons and the blue enamel saucepans to create a kind of French country look. I revived as many of my grandmother's recipes as I could remember: chicken soup, noodle kugel; she even had a special way with chocolate chip cookies.

The years went on and the children came along—two sons in quick succession and then after a five-year break, a third. Then came renovations and a move to a larger home, and with each one, a bigger, more up-to-date kitchen. The tattersall wallpaper faded and was replaced; the plank with S-hooks came down to make way for new windows. We bought a long, sturdy, oak butcher block table that held special significance for me, becoming the place of nightly dinners for our expanding family. On Friday nights, I lit candles and served Shabbat dinners where each son recited a blessing, with the youngest boy always selected to blow out the match.

Some years later, with Bill's real estate business doing well, we moved to a larger house even farther from the city.

This house had a completely up-to-date kitchen, with every pullout drawer and as much counter space as I could ever want. I couldn't have hung the old pot rack on the wall even if I wanted to because the walls were covered by imported Italian tiles, hand-selected by the previous owner.

It was a dream come true, that kitchen. But less than two years after we moved into that house, the marriage ended.

When the house was put up for sale as a part of the divorce, I was surprised to find how little I minded the loss of our showy "dream house." We had not been happy there. I had never been comfortable with how far away the children's rooms were from my room, located in a separate master wing. The swimming pool I always wished to have one day had turned out to be a royal nuisance, with a propane heater that constantly needed reigniting and a surface that continually needed to be cleaned of dead leaves when the boys wanted to swim. The house itself was so impressive in size, I suspected every serviceman of immediately doubling his estimate as soon as he drove up the circular drive. The tennis court meant nothing to me, never having learned to play. With my marriage now collapsing, I wondered what had possessed us to move here. Who had we been trying to impress . . . and to what end?

But I did mourn the prospect of losing my big, beautiful kitchen. I tried to stay away when real estate agents led prospective buyers through its roomy expanse, pointing out the top-of-the-line appliances and designer hardware.

On one of my teary phone calls to my mother, I

lamented the loss of our home and most of all, that dream kitchen.

My mother had an immediate response. "Jessica," she said, "don't you realize? Any kitchen of yours will be wonderful."

Well, of course she's going to have something comforting to say, I thought, quick to dismiss what sounded like yet another well-meaning but unhelpful "You're going to be all right" comment. For months now these pat phrases had readily poured forth from a plethora of sympathetic friends and how-to-get-divorced books but had rarely managed to lift my mood. After my mother's phone call, I stopped to reflect. *Any kitchen of mine? What does that mean?*

I thought back on all my kitchens over the years. I thought about how much had changed from one to the other and how much had not changed. Certain items had followed me from the pegboard-walled student apartment, to the tiny walk-in high atop Manhattan, and eventually to the big designer kitchen. There were the few pots and casserole dishes I had inherited from my grandmother's Bronx row house, cheaply made but which I treasured far more than the designer cookware. The odd finds collected over the years at tag sales, like a bread board made from a pullout wooden drawer shelf. My stained aprons and the constant procession of burnt oven mitts that I mostly forgot to use anyway.

But mostly, of course, what my kitchens all had in common was . . . me. Me with my imperfect timing that inevitably resulted in dishes arriving from stove to table in a kind of staggered procession so that my sons came to think of pasta as dessert. Me who would never settle for a single reassurance that my meal was good, but could never help repeating, sometimes two or more times, "How is everything?" "Do you like it?" "Are you sure you like it?" I was entirely aware that whether or not they really were enjoying what was served to them, Bill and the children would give me the answers they knew I wanted: "Really delicious!" or "Great dinner, Mom!" I didn't care. Their praise satisfied me more than the food ever could.

Yes, every one of my kitchens had been wonderful. And I had always found serenity in my kitchens, even during the most difficult years of the marriage. But it wasn't the mixing spoons or the fancy enamel pots that had given me the most pleasure. What had always mattered most was the deep, unexplainable satisfaction I found from nourishing the people I loved. I always discovered a way to cater to the particular needs and tastes of each one—French fries for my brothers long ago, creative and colorful vegetarian meals for Bill, the special ice-cold Russian soup known as *schav* for my mother because I was the only one who could make it exactly like her mother did, the ravioli cooked with *no* sauce for David and *with* sauce for Rob, the carefully screened baby food for my allergic youngest son Alex.

If each of my kitchens did have one thing in common, it was this—a table where my family—and yes, I would still always have family—would find a meal or a dish served just the way they liked it. Reassuring them always, in a steady and unspoken way, that they were treasured for the individuals they were, and that they were loved.

Whatever new kitchen wall I would find on which to hang my pictures or my pots, there would always, certainly, be this.

As most divorces do, mine left me in markedly reduced financial circumstances afterward. The house I was able to afford with the proceeds of my share of the marital assets had a small kitchen with cheaply made pressboard cabinets. The Formica countertop had only one small section alongside the stove where I would do all my chopping and food preparation. There was no room for the long butcher block table, which was dismantled and stored in two parts in the attic. Instead of a table, I had a small built-in counter that seated exactly four, placed at an awkward angle to enable it to fit into the small room. Here we would sit so close that the boys could swipe a French fry off each others' plates or place a Brussels sprout on the plate of an unsuspecting brother while they thought I wasn't looking. They would regale me with stories of their weird teachers and nutty things that happened at school, filling the small kitchen with constant laughter. This was also the place where the boys, groggy and silent, would eat a good breakfast, at my insistence, before school.

Alongside the kitchen is a dining room where my sons' high school friends regularly assembled for Saturday poker games. It is the place where we frequently invite friends for bountiful meals, which I somehow always manage to produce from my small kitchen. When holidays come and my mother, stepfather, sister, brothers, and their families squeeze together for Thanksgiving dinner or Passover Seders, there is always, somehow, room for all. And when I stand at the door in my apron and ask, "How is everything?" a chorus of voices of people who love me rise almost in unison and tell me, "Yes, Jessica, every bit of this miraculous meal is most remarkably, most assuredly wonderful!"

A Sense of Direction

In all our trips to foreign cities, my husband was the one to hold the map. He would balance the guidebook and tourist map, peer intently at street posts, and in short order figure out not only our exact location but also how to get from our hotel to the museum; from museum to central piazza, fountain, or notable statue; from cathedral to restaurant (which he had strategically selected the night before from *GaultMillau*); and then back to the hotel. By the second day of any trip he would no longer even be using the map, having "scoped out" the layout of the town, no matter how winding the streets, nor how many corners to turn. My husband, one had to say, had a good sense of direction.

I, on the other hand, with a quite respectable IQ and the ability to mentally compute the dollar value of 282,000 lira (the price of Tanino Crisci suede boots), have no sense of direction whatsoever. Street maps of foreign cities are useless; the tidy diagrams of lettered streets never seem to bear any relationship to the abstract crisscross of converging piazzas, traffic circles, and narrow pathways that once in a while, if a town father had felt charitable, would display a corresponding street sign. So despite my otherwise normally independent nature, I tended to be uncharacteristically complacent about allowing myself to be led around on our vacations. The relaxation afforded by not having to find my way around seemed well worth the surrender of autonomy. Besides which, not having my nose in a map left a lot more time to take in the scenery.

But my day of reckoning came some years after my divorce. Firmly resolving that my single status should not prevent me from indulging my love of foreign travel, I decided to spend a week in one of my favorite cities, Rome. I knew I would not be lonely for a minute in that place of sun-drenched cafés and ancient artifacts and friendly Italians who would point you in any direction you needed to go. This solo trip to Rome would be a week of triumph, I decided. I would celebrate that after years of marriage, child-rearing, and a dreary divorce, my spirit of adventure and my old self-confidence were intact.

I arrived one morning on a day of bright early spring Italian sunshine. After leaving my luggage unpacked in my hotel room and a quick lunch in the hotel café, I set out. I was on a mission: From my hotel situated in the Piazza della Rotonda, I would head directly for the Trevi Fountain. I wanted to return to the scene of a photograph taken many years before, when I had first fallen in love with Rome.

It was a photograph taken during my first trip to Europe in 1974, the summer after college. In the photo, three of us are seated close together, laughing, on the edge of the Trevi Fountain—two young men, college classmates of mine, with me in between. That year, it had seemed that the entire American and Canadian college-age population, like me, was spending the summer roaming Europe with a backpack, the *Let's Go Europe* guide, and a fifty-six dollar unlimited student rail pass. I had run into the two boys at a student hostel the previous week in Florence. Although I knew them only slightly, the three of us, with no advance planning, decided to travel together to Rome.

It was an unforgettable week. We wandered through museums, dashed across hot, busy intersections, and indulged in long, giddy picnics of summer fruits, cheese, and inexpensive Italian wine. I also spent the time trying to decide which boy I felt more attracted to and admit to considerable flirting. We parted ways after seven days, leaving me with memories that never fail to reawaken the joyful sense of being young, footloose, and heady with romance.

Twenty-five years later, that old sense of romance reawakened as I crossed the piazza with the warm sun on my shoulders. I turned down a shady side street and then, within minutes, it happened. I was lost.

According to the map furnished at my hotel's front desk, the Trevi Fountain was no more than ten or twelve blocks away—using the term *blocks* loosely to describe its abstract sketch of lines and curves that held not one right-angled corner. Staring at the map to orient myself,

I peered at a plaque on the side of a stone building—was this a street sign or commemoration of some historic event?—and walked half a block. After searching for another street sign, I swiveled my body, then swiveled the map. "Right, then left, then another left at that big square-ish area," I muttered. But after that first right turn, I forgot the entire sequence and somehow found myself on a street that was not supposed to be there. Back to the map to begin again.

To complicate matters, Roman street names, I later realized, have a way of changing for no discernible reason. If I had been only moments before heading correctly up the Via del Seminario, why did I suddenly, without so much as a swivel, find myself on the Via Maddalena? Where in the world was Via Maddalena, and where was I? So there I was on my first day in Rome, not a triumphant, independent woman at all, but a pathetic figure with guide books slipping out from under one arm, blundering along, muttering aloud to herself, glasses off to squint at the street signs, glasses on to read the map. (I hadn't needed reading glasses twenty-five years ago, I realized.)

Asking for directions (Bill would have gone to Asia before resorting to asking for directions) barely helped. This was not very difficult in Italian: "Dovè' Fontana di Trevi?" The answer was usually the same: a long indecipherable discourse and a finger pointing straight ahead accompanied by the word *sinestra*. Without much Italian, I nevertheless did know that *sinestra* does not mean straight ahead but left. So why were they pointing straight ahead?

I happened upon a visual cue that would keep me

READER/CUSTOMER CARE SURVEY

We care about your opinions! Please take a moment to fill out our online Reader Survey at **http://survey.hcibooks.com.**
As a **"THANK YOU"** you will receive a **VALUABLE INSTANT COUPON** towards future book purchases
as well as a **SPECIAL GIFT** available only online! Or, you may mail this card back to us.

(PLEASE PRINT IN ALL CAPS)

First Name	MI.	Last Name

Address		City

State	Zip	Email

1. Gender
❑ Female   ❑ Male

2. Age
❑ 8 or younger
❑ 9-12   ❑ 13-16
❑ 17-20   ❑ 21-30
❑ 31+

3. Did you receive this book as a gift?
❑ Yes   ❑ No

4. Annual Household Income
❑ under $25,000
❑ $25,000 - $34,999
❑ $35,000 - $49,999
❑ $50,000 - $74,999
❑ over $75,000

5. What are the ages of the children living in your house?
❑ 0 - 14   ❑ 15+

6. Marital Status
❑ Single
❑ Married
❑ Divorced
❑ Widowed

7. How did you find out about the book?
(please choose one)
❑ Recommendation
❑ Store Display
❑ Online
❑ Catalog/Mailing
❑ Interview/Review

8. Where do you usually buy books?
(please choose one)
❑ Bookstore
❑ Online
❑ Book Club/Mail Order
❑ Sports
❑ Price Club (Sam's Club, Costco's, etc.)
❑ Retail Store (Target, Wal-Mart, etc.)

❑ Christianity
❑ Spirituality/Inspiration
❑ Business Self-help
❑ Women's Issues
❑ Sports

9. What subject do you enjoy reading about the most?
(please choose one)
❑ Parenting/Family
❑ Relationships
❑ Recovery/Addictions
❑ Health/Nutrition

10. What attracts you most to a book?
(please choose one)
❑ Title
❑ Cover Design
❑ Author
❑ Content

TAPE IN MIDDLE; DO NOT STAPLE

BUSINESS REPLY MAIL

FIRST-CLASS MAIL PERMIT NO 45 DEERFIELD BEACH, FL

POSTAGE WILL BE PAID BY ADDRESSEE

Health Communications, Inc.
3201 SW 15th Street
Deerfield Beach FL 33442-9875

FOLD HERE

Comments

oriented—a building with a neon green first aid cross out front that I figured must be a hospital. But no matter which direction I walked, I kept arriving just down the street from neon green cross. Which obviously meant I was going in circles.

This went on for about two hours that first day at which point, totally defeated, I slumped against the window of an electronics store. Self-pity and jet lag turned to tears. It was hopeless. With my dismal sense of direction, I concluded, I would never figure out how to get around on my own. At best, I would spend this week missing everything on the way to my intended destinations because I would see nothing but the street map. Dejected, I briefly considered giving up on trying to see Rome at all this week. Maybe I should just spend all my time at the Café della Rotonda right in front of my hotel, I thought, indulging in a few moments of feeling sorry for myself.

Then reason took hold, and I wiped the tears off my reading glasses. No. I did not come to Rome to sit in a café. I wanted to see the Coliseum again. I wanted to stand before the Palace of Victor Emmanuel on the far side of the city, where my two long-ago college companions had teased me that the statues were real and then chucked me under the chin when I believed them. I would tackle this problem tomorrow. I would develop a sense of direction, this very week. With a new and better map.

Giving up on the Trevi Fountain—for now—I headed back to my hotel.

With new resolve and a good night's sleep behind me,

I began my next day by purchasing a bigger, easier-to-read map. I plotted my course and paid close, fierce attention. End of the block, check map, turn. There was the Piazza Navona, just where the map showed it would be. At times I challenged myself to put away my map and head in what seemed to be the correct general direction. This always turned out to be a bad idea. But I did soon enough learn not to rely on green neon first aid cross signs as route markers. These, I belatedly discovered, were not attached to one single hospital at all. Instead they were the universal Italian sign for a pharmacy. There was a green neon cross displayed on the window or doorway of every drugstore in Rome.

With my new map, I accurately managed to find my way to the Palazzo del Quirinale and was now headed back. So far so good. I was footsore and tired, but at least I knew that the street I was on would eventually lead to my hotel. Then I made a sudden, unplanned stop. My attention had been captured by a display of gorgeous, intricately decorated chocolate Easter eggs, nestled in marzipan nests, in the window of a corner confectionery store. I had to go inside and get a closer look. Inside the store, after admiring an array of Easter eggs and marzipan animals in their glass case, I carefully selected three eggs to bring home to my boys. But then, as I paid my bill and turned to leave, I once again stopped short. The shop had not one but two exit doors, adjacent to each other but catty-corner, so that each opened onto to a different street. I had been so captivated by the candy eggs when I entered that I had forgotten to take note of which of the two doors I used. I chose one door at random and came out onto an unfamiliar corner. Presto! I was lost again.

This time there was nothing to do but stand on that street corner and laugh.

It was the moment of the truth. *All right,* I thought, *so I have no sense of direction. But how badly do I need one, anyway?* After all, I was not some soldier on a military mission—and I never would be. Okay—so I would be my own spectacularly lost self, stumbling, stopping, asking, and pretending to understand complicated Italian directions with a vacant smile and friendly *"Grazie,"* before heading off in the completely wrong direction. And if I didn't get where I wanted to go, well then, I would just see what I would find instead.

Which is exactly what happened during the remainder of a nearly perfect week in Rome. I would begin each day with an unhurried breakfast in the Café della Rotonda, which by now I had made the equivalent of my own Roman front porch. Lingering under the warm Mediterranean sunshine, I took all the time I wanted for a second and then a third cup of coffee. The waiter didn't correct my Italian once. Often a ragtag street violist circled the café, playing his heart out with a melodramatic expression that made up for the scratchy Strauss waltzes.

After breakfast, with my mostly ignored map deep in my purse, I would set out toward some destination I would decide was "over there-ish." One morning I decided to head for the flower-bedecked outdoor market in the Campo dei Fiori, where I hoped to find for lunch the fresh ricotta that I remembered, with its mountain-air sweetness unlike anything to be found at home. After many wrong turns, I took the better part of the morning to get there so it was far beyond lunchtime by the time I entered the Campo dei Fiori. But along the way I happened upon the tiny Café Saint Eustache with its coffee beans spilling from burlap sacks; a half-hidden shop with notebooks, boxes, and writing paper crafted in delicate, jewel-colored Florentine paper; and a shoe store selling exactly the kind of heel pads I needed for new shoes. At the end of the day, back at my café, I had to conclude that these places stumbled upon along wrong turns and inadvertent detours had been a lot more interesting than the actual Piazza Navona, crowded with souvenir stands, or the Trevi Fountain, which I did eventually find only to discover that its nighttime waters now mostly reflected blinding light from the windows of discount shoe stores flanking it on all sides.

I never did get to the Coliseum. But on my last evening in Rome, as I wandered from my hotel for one last stroll, I turned a corner and there, at the end of the Via del Corso where I could have sworn it wasn't supposed to be, was the monumental palace of Victor Emmanuel, gleaming like a wedding cake against a predusk sky of deep aquamarine. I stood for a long time, my heart twisting, as the sky darkened behind the glowing monument with its soaring columns, golden spires, and flank of manly Roman warriors.

I knew then that I had my own special sense of direction. In my version, the markings were not street signs, but emotions stirred by memory. The attractions weren't plaques or piazzas, but the sensual feel of Italian street names on the tongue or the scent of espresso wafting from tiny cafés. My souvenirs that week were not post-cards but adventures freshly gathered, like the time I struck up a restaurant conversation with two German women, travel companions for over forty years, who shared with me stories of their heartaches and photos of their cats. Or when I was befriended after a concert by a young Italian secretary who offered me a ride home in a Fiat not much bigger than the huge golden retriever that panted between us from the back seat.

And best of all, with my very own unique sense of direction, the palace of Victor Emmanuel could appear from out of nowhere, brilliantly white and heart-stop-ping as it had always been, and would always be—high on a hill, *a la sinestra,* and most wonderfully, most unex-pectedly, straight ahead.

Intimacy in Many Forms and Unexpected Places

There's a great moment in the movie *Dead Man Walking* when the convicted prisoner taunts Sister Prejean through the prison bars. "Come on, Sister, don't you miss having a man?" he says with a lewd look. Her face has a soft expression as she answers him.

"I haven't experienced sexual intimacy, but there's other ways of being close . . . sharing your dreams, your thoughts, your feelings. That's being intimate, too."

At the time it struck me that this was an odd subject—*intimacy*—for a nun to be able to speak of with such authority. But in the years following my divorce, it has often occurred to me how apt the word *intimacy* is in describing the new dimension that so many of my relationships assumed when there was no longer a man in my life.

Bill and I had had a fairly large circle of what I would

136

call social acquaintances in our comfortable suburban town: neighbors, parents of our sons' playmates, members of our synagogue. We also socialized with business-related acquaintances to whom we referred as friends but were more like semifriends. The common denominator was that these were friends with whom one kept up one's guard. We greeted them with touched cheeks and air kisses, drank wine with them at Saturday night parties and fund-raisers, and compared children's teachers and soccer coaches over iced tea on Open School Night. In brief, animated conversations, the other mothers and I caught up on what was happening in our children's classrooms or on the outrageous amount a house on someone's street just sold for. We gossiped about whose housekeeper had gotten pregnant and the new shoe store opening in town. The new mothers' playgroup I had formed when David was an infant still got together on Thursday afternoons, even after the children began school. Each dinner party invitation felt like a small triumph: Bill and I were in the club.

But something was missing, and I couldn't figure out what it was. Regardless of how many Saturday nights we laughed over wine with another couple at a local restaurant, regardless of how many other parents I could greet by name or trade jokes with on the Little League bleachers, something about these friendships felt terribly empty. Perhaps if we could just spend more time with each other, I thought, we would eventually become close. Maybe even take a weekend or vacation away together. I arranged numerous dinner parties and jockeyed to be among the couples invited to a restaurant gathering. If I heard of some social occasion to which Bill and I had not been invited, I felt devastated.

Surrounded by so many couples like us, whose lives were so similar to mine, I could find no reason for a persistent sense of loneliness. This was nothing like college, when my friends and I seemed to know each other heart and soul. All I knew was that even at the liveliest dinner party, replete with witty, wine-fueled conversations about politics, our children, or stories in the *New York Times*, I felt disconnected. I concluded that it must be something wrong with me.

No one among this lively, interesting group of young parents or synagogue members could have suspected the awful state of my marriage. No one knew about the tense nights and the silent mornings, the sarcasm and criticism, the recriminations that flew back and forth between Bill and me. This thing that was occupying the front and center place in my soul, that dampened my mood at every trip to the playground or supermarket, every dinner party, every Thursday afternoon playgroup, was my secret. To the other young mothers and the other couples in our social circle, everything looked wonderful. Ideal, almost: a successful couple, thriving business, three bright and well-behaved children, great house.

When word got out that Bill and I had split up, the general reaction was one of disbelief, followed by a kind of arm's length sympathy.

The dinner invitations came to a halt. Restaurant get-togethers were out of the question, since we could no longer occupy our half of a restaurant table that seated four. As for parties, I could imagine my friends' dilemma—

who to invite, Bill or me? It was a likely explanation for why I so quickly became extraneous in our former paired-up social world.

Or perhaps that wasn't the full explanation after all. Because Bill later shared with me that remarkably soon after our separation, his phone began ringing with offers to fix him up with an endless selection of unmarried or divorced friends, daughters, or sisters-in-law. I soon learned that nothing has a shorter "shelf life" than a presentable, wealthy man in an unattached state. I was fairly sure it would not be the same for me, an unattached woman with three young children. Not that I cared. The last thing I had any interest in during those heart-wrenching early days of the separation was dating. I wanted nothing more than to hunker down with my kids.

But without my realizing it, my change in status from married to separated resulted in an even more seismic shift in my social life. The oddest thing began happening. In that first rush of sympathetic phone calls, friends— not just women, but men, too—blurted out to me the most intimate details of their own lives, primarily the problems or doubts they were having in their own marriages. Suddenly the perfect-couple veneer that so many had kept polished, as I had, was stripped away.

It was mind-boggling. I was fascinated that my own admission of a failed marriage seemed to have transformed other people's perception of me into a sympathetic recipient for these highly personal revelations. Somehow, in publicly announcing my unhappy, all-too-imperfect state, I had crossed an invisible border from suburban icon to approachable human being. I had somehow become someone to whom people not only *could* reveal their own vulnerabilities, but were *hungry* to.

I felt a little like a doctor at a cocktail party to whom, once his identity is revealed, people begin recounting their physical ailments. Sometimes even the most casual acquaintances, like mothers waiting with me for their children at the school bus stop, or near strangers like medical receptionists or school secretaries who noticed the "divorced" box checked off, felt compelled to confess to their own marriage dissatisfactions or divorce history with a frankness that was remarkable.

It was a revelation, certainly, to learn that beneath its highly polished surface, all was not rosy in our velvet-walled suburban world. It was a sobering discovery, too, like that moment when the parted curtain reveals that the Wizard of Oz is just an old man with spectacles and a voice amplifier. I took no satisfaction in the knowledge that so many ideal couples were in fact close to the edge. Some small part of me still hoped that marriage could be Happily Ever After—that it might even be one day again, for me.

Aside from the issue of marital unhappiness, these confessions led me to speculate even more. Could other women also have sat at Little League games feeling somehow apart? Had other women been craving, but failing to find, a sense of belonging, just as I had?

The unexpected gift of my divorce was that its announcement seemed to inspire an entirely new, immensely gratifying level of intimacy with the other adults in my world. It was almost exhilarating. Not since my college friends had huddled on each other's dorm room beds trading secrets, heartaches, and dreams late into the night had I experienced the deep pleasure that comes from connecting, truly connecting, with other human beings. Aside from my sister, my mother, and one very close friend, this closeness had rarely existed throughout my adulthood. My deepest secrets I shared with a therapist in expensive, forty-five minute increments. Emotional intimacy was not something Bill and I had shared for years.

It was like another moment in *The Wizard of Oz,* when the entire world changes from black-and-white to Technicolor. For the first time in years, loneliness was gone, as I found myself deeply satisfied by a new and deeper dimension of relating. At the same time, it took surprisingly little effort to discard those relationships that remained shallow. Social invitations from which I was excluded now meant little to me. Not only was I *not* devastated to hear of the party or Bat Mitzvah from which I was excluded, but I was relieved. I no longer had an interest in cocktail party conversations or so-called friendships that never went below the surface. My friendships were fewer, certainly. But they were friendships that mattered.

What happened next was that I developed a wealth of new relationships and friendships. Many of these never would have appeared in my life when I was married.

Not long after the divorce, I spent my week traveling alone in Italy while the boys spent spring vacation with Bill. The first few rapturous days, I took long, sun-drenched walks around Rome, rejoicing in the voluptuous pleasures of the city's art, architecture, and street life. But on the fourth day, I had to admit I was lonely. Dispirited from listening only to traffic noise and the sound of my own voice stumbling over Berlitz-assisted Italian phrases, I began to crave conversation in my own language. I found a solution in a glossy brochure on the hotel's front desk. For an exorbitant price, one could take a one-day, round-trip bus excursion to Naples that included a boat ride, grotto tour, and (of course) a souvenir shopping trip on the Isle of Capri. It was the kind of prepackaged tourist venture Bill would have avoided at all costs. I myself would not have signed up for it, had I not been determined to keep myself from descending into feeling-sorry-for-my-lonely-state or, even worse, depression. How bad could it be? I decided to act like an American tourist and give it a shot.

On the three-hour air conditioned bus trip to Naples, I found myself surrounded by sixteen middle-aged American women who were traveling together and apparently, having a rollicking good time. By the time the bus drew up to the dock in Naples, I had given up on trying to understand the almost incomprehensible patter of the heavily accented tour guide over the loudspeaker, put aside my novel and my journal, and was actively listening in on the women's lively chatter.

As the women boarded the polished wooden launch that would leave from the pier at Naples to Capri, the entire group of sixteen crammed together to try to get a group picture against various backdrops—fishing boats on the pier, Mount Vesuvius in the far distance, and just across the water, the island of Capri with its craggy arches and caves. On an impulse, I spoke up and offered to take the snapshot for them. They cheerfully accepted, asked my name, and by the end of the twenty-five minute boat ride, I was one of the group.

The women turned out to be members of an investment club from Ridgewood, New Jersey, who, despite the fact that they were all rank amateurs, had done surprisingly well with their small pool of investments. As a reward to themselves, they had left husbands behind to take a five-day, fast-paced, all-inclusive package trip to Italy. Everything for these women was an occasion for uproarious laughter: the floppy hat blown into the water, the rocking excursion boat, the hunky, ripe-smelling young Italian men who handed us into small boats for the grotto tour. The women insisted I join them for lunch in a restaurant on Capri after the boat tour, when they were thrilled to learn that I could order for all of us in passable Italian. I looked at pictures of grandchildren and chatted with a recently widowed woman who had been practically forced to come along on the trip and now couldn't help but admit to enjoying herself. Back on the bus at day's end, we admired each other's souvenirs purchased in the open shops that lined the hilly roads of Capri. Someone took my address so she could send me copies of the group photos that by now included me. By the time I begged off having pizza with them back at their hotel in Rome, any lingering loneliness had been dispelled. I was cheered and ready for the next day's quieter visit to the Galleria Borghese.

This kind of thing happened again and again. But it wasn't automatic. I learned that for relationships to develop in this way with such delightful serendipity, a little effort was required on my part. Sometimes it was something as simple as offering to take a photo for tourists, so their group shot could be complete. Sometimes it took more planning, such as the many evenings I forced myself to attend local business networking events, volunteer for a political campaign, or join a women's entrepreneurial organization. In my more upbeat moments, filled with confidence and resolve, I would register online for business luncheons, my college alumni association's networking dinners, and professional development workshops in the area or even in New York City, an hour's train ride away. Many times the day would arrive, finding me too tired to go or with cold feet about facing a room full of strangers. But because my frugality made it impossible to throw away money I had already spent to register for these events, I usually forced myself to go.

There was something more I had to do as well, although I couldn't have defined what this was until much later. To be open to these spontaneous encounters that might become friendships and deepen into relationships, I had to venture out with my "single man" radar firmly turned off. After my separation, even during times I had little interest in a new romantic relationship, I had been annoyed to discover that radar was on. But my other unmarried friends confessed to it, too—a kind of instinctive awareness, when one walked into a room, of whether any of the attractive or interesting-looking men there were unattached, and who might be interested in more than an exchange of business cards. Many single women never turn off that radar. I have often witnessed the lights in their eyes shut off the moment a man is revealed to be married or unavailable. I worked very hard never to let that happen.

One November, I received an announcement that my Chamber of Commerce's holiday party would be a black-tie gala. What did I have to lose, besides fifty dollars and a Saturday night home alone? I sent in my check. And go I did, in a dark red cocktail dress and black silk heels, with an evening bag. Over before-dinner cocktails, I was introduced to the CEO of a local investment firm who, after learning that I had recently left my job as a business editor, asked me to call him on Monday. He later became the first client of my newly hatched public relations firm. I got to dance with the ninety-year-old "boyfriend" of the Chamber president (a much younger woman, barely in her seventies), who waved us onto the dance floor with her blessing. Elegant in his tuxedo, he hummed with a dreamy expression while we danced to Cole Porter.

At dinner I was seated at a table for nine: four couples and me. They turned out to be a friendly bunch, cohorts of a local real estate firm and their spouses who regularly partied together after work. After the last speech by a few Chamber board members, my tablemates insisted that I join them afterward for drinks and live music at a local bar. By now completely chummy with this group, I happily tagged along and sipped my Diet Coke, and over the noise of a live jazz combo, gossiped about various businesspeople in town and traded information with the women on where we had bought our cocktail dresses.

I came to see that the loneliness that lurked when the children were not around was not such a bad thing after all, because fending off loneliness is what inspired me to get off my butt and go do something new and interesting. Every outing wasn't a winner. But many resulted in a surprising wealth of new relationships and sometimes even deep friendships. At the least, when I had the persistence to return again and again to a library book talk or the Democratic Town Committee or the Entrepreneurial Woman's Network, I had the soul-satisfying experience that comes simply from walking into a room and being greeted by friends—male and female, married and unmarried, young and octogenarian—who didn't just know my name, but really—no *really*—wanted to know how I was.

In this way my world has become a cozy and, yes, more intimate place.

The Mother-in-Law Bond

I was carrying on a secret affair.

At first, we wouldn't even dare to telephone. A note here, a holiday card there. Then the unexpected gift, for no particular reason, with a cryptic note. "These gloves looked like they would suit you." "I thought you would find this hand-painted pocket mirror handy; it was made in Italy." With my children acting as unwitting couriers, I would send food treats. "This key lime pie is the best there is." "I remember you liked my honey cake; enjoy this with the family on the holidays."

Gaby wasn't really my mother-in-law anymore, not legally, since the divorce. It was understood, once the neatly stitched seams of my marriage to her son ripped apart, that she and I were no longer to communicate. Her son wanted it that way. I was the enemy now. The outsider.

After Bill and I separated, I didn't question being omitted from Bill's family events—Bar and Bat Mitzvahs of his nieces and nephews, whom I had held as babies; the wedding of Bill's niece, whom I had taken shopping as a young teen. I didn't go to the funerals of relatives and friends who over two decades I had watched soften into old age and come to think of as my own family.

But even Gaby herself seemed to sense something not right about that, when she wrote to me before the big seventy-fifth birthday party that her children were throwing for her, complete with caterer and musicians. In her upright, spidery scrawl, Gaby wrote that she hoped I would understand my not being invited but wanted to let me know that she would look forward to celebrating with me at future happy occasions of my children. The language was slightly formal and carefully worded to obscure any hint of emotion. Even so, I was touched by the note and utterly surprised. Of course I wasn't to be invited. I was persona non grata. In any case, Bill would be there with his new girlfriend.

When Bill had first introduced me to his parents the autumn after my college graduation, I mentioned I had just returned from a summer backpacking alone through Europe. Gaby regarded me with interest. "Well, that's rather plucky of you," she said, in her Queen Elizabeth British accent. Along with the admiration in her glance, I sensed a note of wistfulness.

From that moment, I felt that we had recognized something in each other, which is odd given how dissimilar we were, really. Born in London in the 1920s and now a strong, intelligent force in the family business and her family of four children, Gaby clung to her accent and British customs with the fixed certainty that those were at all times the absolutely correct way of doing all things. I was a college graduate of the 1970s; with my free-flowing long hair, embroidered jeans, and New York City liberal political notions, I regarded Gaby as something of an oddity from a different century.

Perhaps it was because we were so alike, both so opinionated and strong-willed, that during the early years, Gaby and I did not always have an easy time in our relationship. Some months after Bill and I started living together, he took me down to stay several weeks at his parents' winter home in the Virgin Islands. Gaby and I frequently chafed at each other's presence. A hardy British war bride who had married Bill's father directly from the Women's Royal Air Force, she had little patience with my squeamishness about island life. "We bathe in the sea here, no need to waste water on showers, especially in the dry season," she said brightly, pouring milky breakfast tea. (I hated tea and yearned for brewed morning coffee. If I insisted on coffee, she nodded, "By all means, help yourself, there's a jar of Sanka in the cupboard somewhere, though I couldn't promise you how long it's been there.") The first morning after arriving, I asked where I could find an outlet for my hairdryer. Rather than giving me a simple answer, Gaby offered in a crisp boarding school headmistress tone, "No need for that here—we dry our hair naturally in the breeze." Her insistence upon maintaining the English way of doing all things—whether it was holding one's fork upside down in the wrong hand, overcooking a piece of meat until it was like shoe leather, or referring to tea leaves left in the cup as "slops," drove me crazy. At breakfast one morning, I made a comment bemoaning a fifth straight day of rain. Gaby turned to me with impatience, using an English colloquialism I didn't know but whose meaning I had no trouble figuring out. "Don't gridge, Jessica, you're getting a free vacation here." Tactful she was not. I lifted a napkin to my eyes to hide tears while Bill looked on, sympathetic but helpless.

But from her first "plucky" comment, neither of us could help notice a grudging admiration for each other. Gaby had left her London home at seventeen to join the Royal Air Force just before World War II. In the United States, as a British war bride, she had four babies in fairly quick succession, at the same time going into business with her husband importing antiques and porcelain from war-ravaged Europe. I sensed she had always been the real brains behind the business, if not the backbone— doing the books, accompanying her husband on buying trips, and running an antiques store, all while managing to raise four children. When Bill and his siblings spoke of being embarrassed by their mother's failure to properly wrap a friend's gift in store-bought gift wrap, opting instead for wallpaper from leftover sample books, or forgetting to prepare a special meal for the child who had recently declared himself a vegetarian, I restrained myself from shaking my head. Clearly they didn't have a clue how high-pressured her life must have been. This became even more apparent to me when, after I began having children, like Gaby, I found myself supporting my husband's business by handling the books and managing the office, then dashing home to pay the babysitter and feed everyone, stopping for groceries on the way.

As the years went on, it was clear that I had far more in common with Gaby than being married to her son. By nature we both clung to a steely sense that we usually knew better—even when we didn't. We also shared a determined independence that bristled at the slightest insinuation of sexism. Gaby was a woman of incisive intelligence, well-read, and with an opinion on every-thing from horticulture to world politics. I wondered how far in the world she might have gone if, born in a different place and time, she had not been forced to leave school to work to help support her family in war-torn London and escape an oppressive father by joining the military. By age nineteen, she was a Royal Air Force ser-geant commanding a Women's Auxiliary Air Force troop. Her girls, she called them, in fond, frequently recounted stories of her military life.

Perhaps it was mostly what we had in common that kept us at arms' length from each other during the early years of my marriage to her son. We were both too sure of ourselves, too opinionated and strong-willed, to give way to each other's insistence on the absolutely correct way of doing things. If I asked for less well-done meat, the request fell on deaf ears. After I gave birth, I cringed when she doled out advice about how much fresh air and sunshine babies needed every day—it was the English way—despite the frigid outside temperature. We were too polite to be outright adversaries but too guarded to ever be close.

That all changed when her husband of forty-seven

years was dying of cancer. They were very close and losing him would be a huge blow. However, Gaby shoul-
dered his illness with tight-lipped composure—what her
generation (or once again, the British) would brand as
"courage." When in his last days my father-in-law
became too ill to travel a short distance to our home for
a Passover Seder, I offered to relocate the Seder to Gaby's
house. Although I had to stay home at the last minute
with a sick child, I sent over the entire traditional, home-
cooked holiday meal, so her husband could rally himself
just long enough to sit briefly at the table with all his
children and other grandchildren for this one last
beloved holiday ritual. The soup with matzo balls, Gaby
told me gratefully, was one of the last things he had been
able to eat. After his funeral, Gaby finally allowed her
British composure to crack. She held onto me, sobbing.
"I'll never forget that Passover meal you sent over, never."
Something between us had forever changed.

Then Bill and I were divorced, and she and I once
again became adversaries. This time it was not by choice,
but somehow by definition. Bill's family closed ranks
around him, blaming me for the divorce. Years went by,
and I didn't see most of them. My first glimpse of my former in-laws, including Bill's siblings and assorted first
cousins, didn't come until David's Bar Mitzvah, five years
after our separation. It was painful seeing them, remembering how much his family had once been my own family. But after the divorce, by some ridiculous family
decree, I had been permanently disbarred.

But the odd thing was, I missed Gaby. As the years
went by, I missed what had once driven me to distrac-

tion—her long, prattling stories about her Royal Air Force days and antique-foraging travels with her husband just after the war; her firmly voiced opinions over which political candidate had his wits about him; even her insistence on setting a table with dessert spoon and fork placed horizontally, head to toe, at the top of one's plate in the proper British way, even if dessert consisted only of what she called "biscuits," which we called "cookies." I would chuckle when my sons would come back from a dinner with Bill's family, sighing over how Grandma Gaby would insist on napkins on laps, and forks and knives placed on the plate just so, to let the waiter know whether one was finished eating or just taking a pause.

Years went by. Then not long ago, I started hearing something rather shocking from divorced friends: some of them stayed in touch with the families of their former spouses. This was news to me—weren't extended families always considered enemy camps? Apparently not. My friend Donna takes the children to her former in-laws' house for family dinners and Thanksgivings just like before. "Just because Susan divorced you, doesn't mean that we did," said the former father-in-law of my friend Charlie, who always accepted their invitation for Christmas dinner despite the presence there of his former wife and her new husband. *How odd,* I thought at first. *But why not?*

The idea stayed with me. All right, so this was clearly how Bill wanted it. But now with their grandfather gone, and Gaby getting older, I wanted my children to know their grandmother, and know about her and her life, as much as possible. I wanted her to spend more time with her delightful, funny, amazing grandsons than the occasional formal family party or dinner to which Bill brought them.

And I wanted to cook for her. I remembered how much Gaby had loved my cooking. I imagined that Gaby, never an enthusiastic cook herself, could only have been subsisting on carryout for one or the occasional restaurant meal with friends.

The children would be my excuse.

One early spring day, shortly after Gaby returned from winter in Florida and when Bill was away on vacation, I made the phone call. "The boys haven't seen you all winter. Would you like to come have dinner with them Sunday?" With a slight note of hesitation, she accepted. Surely her son could not object to dinner with her grandchildren.

She brought with her a bouquet of mums, handed to me at the door. "Grandma's here," I called up to the boys, who galloped down the stairs to greet her. I made the dishes that I knew she loved—poached salmon and buttered potatoes with parsley, steamed in the English way. The boys stayed at the table for a long time, and over dessert, key lime pie with whipped cream, she filled them in on her most recent travel adventures. In her seventies and even into her eighties, Gaby never gave up her annual cruise to some different exotic port.

After the children left the table, Gaby and I remained, I with my second cup of coffee, she with her tea. Gaby gently set down her fork with a look of pleasure mixed with sadness. "You know, this is the first home-cooked meal I've had in years," she said. It struck me how poignant it was that this woman, who made a cross-Atlantic trip on the Queen Elizabeth 2 each year and often dined at a country club or at expensive resorts, should be so grateful for this meal.

At the door, I gave her a quick, casual kiss on the cheek. "I hope you'll come again," I said. She hesitated, looked at me quickly, then looked away. "You have to understand, I just can't go against my son's wishes," Gaby said to me, her voice wavering. Yes, of course I understood.

But she did come again, in a series of clandestine dinners that we referred to as "dinner with her grandchildren." No meal was missing her special favorite dessert, the key lime pie she had learned to love during her Virgin Island winters with her late husband. Every time I set one in front of her at the end of a meal, her face would brighten, as though she were newly surprised each time that someone remembered she loved key lime pie. I would serve it to her with a cup of hot, strong English tea, leaving plenty of room for the milk I heated separately.

The boys were always there, of course. That was our excuse. But after dinner when they had gone back to the TV or their homework, Gaby and I would stay at the table a little longer. Gaby brought me up to date on how a cousin in Bournemouth was doing or explained a disagreement among members of the tenant association of her Florida condominium. I pumped her for gossip about distant family members I hadn't heard about for years— a brother in Australia, the children and grandchildren of

Bill's aunt and uncle in Long Island, her cousins in Ottawa. At other times she would recount yet another fascinating story about her travels with her husband— the long deserted road to buy black opals in Lightning Ridge, Australia; their discovery of the last complete set of Royal Worcester china to be found in England after the war; a glass factory in Czechoslovakia; the tea dances during her London childhood where her parents had danced every Saturday without fail. Eventually, I started playing her recordings of my most recent radio commentaries.

Between our dinners, when she wasn't away on a cruise or trip, the occasional card or package would arrive in the mail—from Gaby, gloves or a delicate manicure item; from me, Mother's Day cards signed by her grandsons and flowers on her birthday.

Gaby is well into her eighties now. Her mind is as sharp as ever, her opinions crisp and well-informed. Her formerly brisk English pace is a bit slower, but not by much. Whether or not my sons are in town, she is not a stranger in my home. I love having her in my life.

I'm hoping her son will forgive us.

L'Eclipse

nyone who has ever witnessed a full solar eclipse
will tell you the same thing: you spend the rest
of your life trying to see another.

So the summer after Bill moved out, when I came
across a small notice in a magazine that a full solar eclipse,
billed as the last eclipse of the twentieth century, would
be visible across central Europe in August 1999, I knew I
had to be there. Not only that—I would take the boys. It
would be the perfect way to show them that life would go
on. But more than that, I thrilled at the idea of giving my
sons this gift that would become a lifelong memory—the
awesome spectacle of a full solar eclipse. My sons were
then too young to understand or care what an eclipse was.
Nevertheless, I promised them—or in truth, not so much
promised them but myself—that when that far off day
came, I would take them to Europe to see it.

For over twenty-five years, I had treasured this

indelible memory myself. One weekend in 1968, my brother Eric, an amateur astronomer who later became a genuine eclipse-chaser and witness of many eclipses, drove home with friends from the University of Michigan where he was a student. They had come east for the specific purpose of viewing a rare eclipse that would be visible along the United States Eastern Seaboard. Virginia Beach, another eight-hour drive away, was directly in the path of totality—the maximum phase when the sun goes completely black. There was an extra seat in the car, and my brother unexpectedly invited me to come along on the trip. An unsophisticated fifteen-year-old more awestruck by the presence of college boys than celestial events, I accepted without understanding what we were going to see, or why.

My brother, his shaggy-haired roommate Nick, and a boy from Ohio whose name he had pulled out of the ride box took turns driving throughout the night. I drifted in and out of sleep in the backseat, my eyes resting from time to time on Nick's wide shoulders and dark blond hair as he drove the Philadelphia to Washington, D.C., leg. When Eric stopped the car at four o'clock in the morning at a closed gas station in Delaware to change drivers, a police cruiser pulled up behind us, lights flashing. The car was searched, our IDs scrutinized, and we were sent on our way.

We arrived in Virginia just before six and had breakfast in a nearly empty seaside diner. From across the table, I sneaked surreptitious glances at Nick, noticing for the first time how handsome he was, tall and slow moving, with hair the color of maple. A bookish, awkward high school girl, I had never had a boyfriend, not so much as a date. I had just about given up thinking that kind of thing would ever happen to me. I spoke little.

When we arrived at the beach it was brilliantly sunny and unseasonably warm for early April. The sky was blue and completely clear—perfect for viewing an eclipse. Nick and I somehow found ourselves walking together on the sand. To look directly at the sun would risk permanent eye damage, so Eric had cut up and brought with him nearly opaque pieces of exposed photographic film through which to see the sun change shape. But even better, someone had set up a twelve-inch reflective celestial telescope from which was projected onto white cardboard a miraculously perfect, detailed image of the slowly eroding sun, with bits of white flame licking out from its remaining curve.

While Eric stayed by the telescope engaged in conversation with the other amateur astronomers, Nick and I walked along the beach, picking up shells and bits of crab. From time to time we would stop, struck by something very odd happening to the shadows. As the moment of totality grew nearer, the shadows of every leaf and flower, every shrub, every dried crab shell on the sand were all turning from their original shapes to smaller and smaller crescents. Gradually, they were shrinking to mere slivers. The air had an eerie stillness to it, like the air in a dream. Seagulls, insects, even the ocean seemed to be quieting.

Nick told me about himself and the farm in Ada, Michigan, where he and his five sisters and brothers grew up. He was an artist, he said, and loved to paint as well as make cartoon drawings of comical characters with fantastic inventions. For long periods we did not speak at all as we walked along the water, taking in the muffled sound of the ocean.

It was almost totality, that moment when the sun would turn black. Everyone had gathered around the telescope. The sky turned red brown more quickly by the moment. Nick took my hand. "Look," he said and pointed to the ocean. The entire ocean had turned red. Then suddenly, from out of the sky, long undulating vertical black rods appeared, wriggling like giant serpents from the surface of the water straight up to the sky.

And then, just in that final moment before the moon covered the sun, we turned our faces upward—it was safe to look up, then—just in time to see a brief, brilliant explosion of red, blue, yellow, green, and gold, like fireworks, burst out of the sun, then quickly disappear, almost before I realized what I had just seen. And then the moon slipped fully into place, and the sun became a huge black disk with white fire splaying out behind it. It was totality—the moment in which the sun is blocked, but not completely. Around it the corona glowed fiercely, as if to affirm that there was no blocking the sun entirely, that there never would be; that it would be there, the center around which the Earth gravitated, the source of life without which there would be no survival, no sea, no vegetation, no Nick holding my hand, no me nor Eric, standing on the beach in Virginia, silent, our faces turned to the sky.

All the way home to New York, Nick and I kissed in the backseat. They were my first kisses, stirring, soft, and sweet.

You never read about a burst of color from the sun at the moment of eclipse totality. I don't know if anyone else has ever seen it or if it has ever been documented. The only ones who saw it were Nick and me. After he returned to college in Michigan, Nick sent me a small oil painting he made for me, of the sun going behind a disk of black, with a burst of colors shooting out from one side. I only saw Nick once again after that, on a visit to my brother in Michigan. We exchanged a few letters, but those eventually ended.

I have kept Nick's painting near me my entire life, in my college dorm, my first apartment, over my desk where I write. I kept the painting as a promise, perhaps, that I would one day relive that awesome event indelibly engraved in my memory. But it was about the promise of love, too. The painting always reminded me of what for so long I had thought I would never, could never, have. But on the miraculous day of the eclipse, for the first time, I had.

Now so many years later, even though the 1999 solar eclipse was four years away, it was not too soon to start planning our trip. But where to go? I searched astronomy magazines and websites, finally discovering a NASA site dedicated to the solar eclipse of 1999. It offered a grainy map of Europe bisected with a thick shaded line that traced the path of totality.

After the children were in bed at night, I studied the NASA site. The moon's umbral shadow, it showed, would begin in the North Atlantic and touch down on Earth off the southwestern coast of England. A full view of totality would creep across the Cornwall Peninsula and the Normandy coast. It would cross the English Channel and make landfall in northern France, sweeping through the French countryside, passing thirty kilometers north of Paris and through the Champagne region to the west. Like a swift serpent the shadow would travel a path across southern Belgium, Luxembourg, the Rhine Valley in Germany, and Vienna, Austria. Then on to Hungary, Yugoslavia, Romania, Turkey, and the Black Sea coast of Turkey. The shadow would arrive at Iran's western boundary and then spend the next half hour crossing sparsely populated mountain ranges and deserts before entering Pakistan and skirting the shores of the Arabian Sea. Making its last appearance on Earth in the Bay of Bengal, it would then race back into space, not to return until the next millennium. The entire trip across three continents would have taken approximately two and a half hours.

God's finger tracing the Earth in a swift, dark line.

But where to go? *Sky & Telescope* magazine recommended a cruise in the Black Sea, where the weather was most likely to be clear and dry, the best conditions for viewing totality. No, I could not take three children to Turkey. Somewhere more familiar. Certainly not the southern coast of England, where the sky was always gray and thick with rain clouds. France—yes—Paris! But in Paris, where the path of totality lay thirty kilometers north, there would only be partial viewing. We had to go where the full drama would take place, where the sun would become a black disk. Then I came across the following intriguing mention: "The center line will cut through the city of Metz, whose citizens will witness a total eclipse lasting two minutes and fourteen seconds, provided the winds of good fortune bring clear skies."

That was it. Metz. Wherever it was. In five years, my boys and I would be there to experience that moment when the sun would turn black for two minutes, fourteen seconds, and day would turn to night.

I planned the trip. We would fly to Paris, then travel two and a half hours east by train to the little-known city of Metz, situated two-thirds of the way between Paris and the Rhine. It seemed to be a relatively undistinguished town, with the Cathédrale Saint-Étienne de Metz, a gothic cathedral built between the thirteenth and sixteenth centuries (Metz's only feature apparently worth a mention in the *Michelin Guide*). We would find a hotel. But all we would really need was a place from which to look up at the sky at exactly 12:24 PM. My sons would be awestruck to see the sun turn into a black disk, with its white corona blazing across an unnaturally dark sky. They would remember it their whole lives.

The Novotel Metz Hauconcourt was a small, commercial highway hotel off Autoroute 14, twelve kilometers outside Metz. Fairly nondescript, it normally catered to business travelers or families who needed a stopover on a long vacation trip, which explained the video game in the lobby and swimming pool out back. But on the day we arrived, one day before the eclipse, the hotel had become a happy madhouse, a cacophony of French and German. No one spoke English other than us and a British family.

It turned out that the advent of a full solar eclipse was the most important commercial event to occur in the city of Metz in decades. I was amused to read that there would be a mass viewing of the eclipse in the town square as well as the sports stadium, as though it were something you needed good seats for, rather than simply looking up at the sky. I decided that the boys and I would not to go into town, but instead stay at the hotel, with this smattering of unrelated strangers who had gathered from so many different places for the same momentous reason. We would be the only Americans.

The day arrived. The boys and I were up early; just before seven o'clock in the morning, I stepped outside. The sky, a pearly gray, did not look promising.

Plenty of time for it to clear up, I tried to reassure myself. Surely, the sky will clear by noon.

It was evident that the hotel was not accustomed to huge crowds. The staff was frazzled and overwhelmed, and the food in the breakfast buffet ran out early. The hostess and restaurant manager scrambled around the dining room balancing two and three platters at a time. Even the hotel manager, in a business suit, pitched in.

A little before eleven o'clock, the boys and I stepped out onto the patio. But something was terribly, terribly wrong. Here by the poolside, the air was chilly. Drops of rain blew lightly on my face. *No,* I thought, *this can't be.* I tried to assure myself that there was plenty of time for the sky to clear—almost two hours until the moment of totality. Certainly enough time. Was that a tantalizing wash of blue sky to the east? Or was the sky becoming more overcast by the minute? I tried not to look up too often.

My children ran out to play tag on the lawn leading from the hotel to the highway's edge. They darted between trees and, laughing, wrestled each other to the ground. Three pale-haired German children, oblivious to the chill air, romped and splashed in the pool as though this was any other family vacation. From time to time couples would stroll out of the hotel, squint up at the drizzling sky, murmur quietly, then retreat back inside.

There was nothing to do now but wait. I searched the milky sky and then looked down at the concrete. Where were the shadows? There should have been shadows visible—shadows of my chair, the poplars overhead, the arborvitae lining the paths. But there were no shadows because the sky was still thickly overcast. I glanced at my watch. If there had been shadows, they would by now be turning into crescents. I could picture those crescents sprinkled on the sidewalk at Virginia Beach, cast by the shrinking overhead sun.

The boys ran up to me, red-faced and panting. "Mom, we need some paper. Do you have any paper and a pen? We're going to play dots." This was a game where you connected dots on a page into boxes, one line at a time, with the winner being the person who assembled the most boxes. The three boys crowded around a plastic chair next to mine, making it into a table upon which they began their game. Alex, the youngest and always the one left out, fought to be able to take a turn. "It's a two-person game," said Robert. "You'll get your turn next."

A drop of rain. Then another. No, it was impossible. Was all of western Europe, maybe even Asia, clouded over? It was simply impossible to have traveled so far, waited all these years to once more experience that most profound moment, only to find myself sitting here in a raincoat, alongside the pool in a roadside motel, under a thick, white sky that revealed nothing of the celestial drama above it.

The drops became thicker. I refused to go inside, as though failing to acknowledge the rain would make it simply not so. My children continued their boisterous game of dots, laughing and shoving each other out of the way, ignoring the drops of water from the sky that smeared their inked boxes.

It could stop any minute, I thought, panicking. We had missed the crescents, but there was still time for the clouds to blow over before totality.

This was all wrong. My sons would miss the miracle. They would not be able to have the memory to carry with them throughout their lives. But they weren't showing any concern. Instead they were laughing over their silly game, shoving each other aside, singing nonsense songs. It made no sense.

Occasionally guests from the hotel would wander out onto the patio, hold out an upward palm to check for drops from overhead and retreat inside, speaking softly. Only an elderly man and his wife remained at the patio, under umbrellas. The man's face wore an expression of bitterness. All the other adults seemed to be nonchalant, shrugging philosophically, sharing a rueful laugh. The children were oblivious.

Twenty minutes to go. People had moved their chairs to the lawn, choosing positions. Many spread blankets on the grass and at the same time, opened umbrellas. I took a long time deciding where to place our chairs—

under a tree to shield us from the drops of rain or out on the lawn where we could have an unobstructed view of the sky? On the other side of the field, alongside the highway, three cows moved slowly, chewing grass. The hotel manager and two waitresses began running around, setting up torchieres that looked as though they had been left over from some Tahiti night. Soon they came out with boxes from which they hurriedly passed out thick black eye shields, like aviator glasses but without ear pieces.

I looked up. The sky was impossibly, definitely, thickly grey, the clouds fixed and unrelenting. What in the world was the hotel staff doing, handing out those eye shields? Did they know something that I did not?

And then, as quickly as though a lamp had been switched off, it became dark. Not dark like night or even dusk; instead the low sky turned a strange, eerie brown, and above the highway, an inky purple. The mysterious umbral shadow, the rare mastery of the moon over the sun, had touched Metz. Sodium lights along the highway came on in the low purple sky. The dark lay heavily upon us. People became still and the talking stopped; even the babies were quiet. A few people walked through the brown air with hands outstretched, as though trying to feel the strange atmosphere unlike any we had ever seen.

I knew it was up there, above the thick cloud cover, where I couldn't see it—that black disk with its corona, that burst of light and color that Nick and I had gasped at, and then turned to each other with speechless awe. It was up there, I knew it! Right there above us. And yet, hidden.

I don't know how long the sky was brown and purple like that, the day turned to eerie night. To me, NASA's two minutes and fourteen seconds had seemed like a long afternoon—or perhaps just a few terrible moments—in which my hopes slipped away. And then the pale light came on, just like that, as abruptly as a lamp being switched back on.

It was over. People gathered up chairs and blankets and headed back to the hotel. Babies were scooped up, fathers shrugged with philosophical half-smiles. Children headed back for the swimming pool, peeling off sweatshirts in the chilly air. Slowly the elderly man and his wife folded their chairs and went inside.

"That was awesome, Mom, really it was," said David, coming over to me. It was good of him, I thought absently, but of course, he couldn't mean it. He was just saying it to make me feel better.

"No," I said, dully. "No, it wasn't."

David went back to his brothers who were swinging their umbrellas. I put my face in my hands and cried.

The realization that it was over, irrevocably, irreversibly over, rolled on top of me like a boulder. How could this be, how could this be? After all the miles traveled, the reservations and the faxes and the hours spent on the telephone with airlines and desk clerks and travel agents. But certainly the other guests in this hotel, now so matter-of-factly heading back to the luncheon buffet, had done the same to witness this eclipse. They must surely be disappointed, too. I couldn't understand why I was the only one to have remained here in the meadow, crying in the soft rain. There seemed to be something intensely personal about this loss that belonged to me alone.

It was about more than the miles we had traveled to be here. It was about the years. My teen and my college and my young adult and my mature years—a failed marriage behind me and an uncertain future in front of me. Perhaps love was, after all, behind me forever. My small painting held a promise unfulfilled.

The NASA website had indicated that there would be more full solar eclipses in the next century, visible over places such as Antarctica and Africa. But the next one occurring over anywhere I would be likely to travel to would be 2082. I would be dead by then. This had been my last chance.

For the rest of the day, I couldn't shake my depression. Listlessly, I wondered how we would fill the rest of the afternoon in this un-noteworthy town, until our return to Paris the next day. There was a small amusement park nearby, the desk clerk told me; but when we headed for it in our rented Fiat I took a wrong turn and ended up in the center of Metz.

We found the village in the midst of celebration. Cutouts of moons, suns, and stars, sprinkled with glitter, dangled from every streetlight and from wires strung across intersections. Narrow cobblestone streets wove between old stone houses that seemed unchanged for two hundred years. The houses were faded but with bright green and blue off-kilter shutters and flower boxes. A marching parade representing every European nation surged through the narrow streets. Clowns dressed as moons lurched on huge stilts two stories high,

while huge, inflated balloons meant to look like clouds—
How fitting, I thought gloomily—squeezed through narrow passes and bounced off heads of laughing and
applauding parade viewers. Leggy women with spangled
leotards and huge Mardi Gras orange feathers splaying
from their backs represented glamorous suns. The
onlookers were in a celebratory mood, crowding the
sidewalks, cheering as each new representation of a
celestial object cruised by.

To these happy crowds, the eclipse seemed to be no
more than an excuse, like Bastille Day, for a huge town
party. I was mystified. Was no one else aware of the
colossal disappointment that had befallen us that day? I
forced myself to look up. The sun now shone innocently
in a cruelly blue and cloudless sky.

My children and I found a tiny table among the cafés
clustered in the medieval central town square and
ordered ice cream sundaes. Metz was certainly not what
I had expected. The cathedral was a towering, lacy wonder of thirteenth century terra-cotta that soared two
hundred feet above us. Every inch of the huge square
was crowded with revelers—families with toddlers and
children digging into bowls of ice cream and yanking
apart pastries, teenagers sharing laughs and cigarettes,
men and women clustered around huge frosty pitchers
of beer, and teenage girls in tight pants and pink lip gloss
flirting with skinny boys astride parked mopeds.

My sons were now deeply involved in their ice cream
sundaes. Not sure whether I was addressing them or
myself, I sighed. "You know," I said, attempting to sound
convincing, "it's funny how things work out sometimes.

We couldn't find that amusement park we were looking for. So from getting lost, we actually ended up somewhere better."

"Well, Mom, that's one way to look at it," said David, intently digging for chocolate chips from his sundae with a long-stemmed spoon. "Or maybe there's just something really great going on *everywhere,* all the time. And it's just a question of which one you happen to end up at, at any particular time."

I looked at my fourteen-year-old son. Then I turned to the crowds of tables, the streamers from the brightly shuttered windows, the silly glitter and glue suns and stars dangling from streetlights, the sunlight glinting off the filigree cathedral spire, the rivulets of moisture that dripped down beer pitchers and wine carafes as they passed from hand to hand. Then I turned back to my sons. Curly-haired Robert was digging into his ice cream with a pirouette wafer, while Alex was using his tongue to catch chocolate fudge dripping down the sides of his bowl.

It occurred to me, then, how little time remained before my three sons would no longer be little boys playing dots and swinging umbrellas in an open field. Something good going on every place, David had said. Yes, and every time, too. There would never again be this time.

My eyes stung, but this time, I held back the tears.

Back in Paris, there was still much to do. There was the military museum in the Hôtel des Invalides where the boys sat astride cannons, pretending they were horses. A quick Metro ride took us to the Picasso Museum, in which the boys had no interest whatsoever but stayed outside on the patio doing fantasy role-playing games. As a bribe for agreeing to a quick visit to the Cezannes in the Museé d'Orsay I promised Alex one last visit to the Eiffel Tower where the Senegalese bird man sold windup plastic birds for exorbitant tourist prices.

On the way home from the Eiffel Tower, I noticed I was out of film. The boys waited on a park bench while I ran into a camera store.

"Do you work nearby?" asked the camera store clerk, as he rang up my two rolls of film.

I looked at him, surprised. Had my French gotten so good in just ten days that I might have been mistaken for local? "No," I said, "I am a visitor. A tourist."

"Ah," he said and then persisted. "Vacation? Are you traveling alone?" The young man was looking at me with interest. He was nice looking, with short dark hair. Probably a good deal younger than I. Then it struck me. This young man was flirting with me.

"No, I came with my children. We came to see the eclipse," I said, stumbling a little in my French that suddenly became more awkward than before. I went on to recount what had happened. "But it was cloudy—you know—we didn't see anything," I said. Even now, there was sadness in my voice.

The young man watched me intently and then tilted his head just a tiny bit, as though considering something. When I finished speaking, he looked down with a shy smile. He reached beneath his counter and brought up a glossy photograph. It was a gleaming black sky and pulsing out from it, a blazing white corona around a sun of solid black. A perfect photo that captured the moment of totality in all its most vivid and awesome splendor.

"You took this?" I said, with a deep breath. "It's perfect. Amazing. Are you a photographer?"

He shrugged. "An amateur."

He lifted the photograph and very carefully placing it into a white envelope, handed it to me. "Here, this is for you," he said, with a soft smile, a small shrug, and a wistful look.

I keep the photograph framed, over my desk, like a promise.

Twice the Work, Four Times the Fun

I was at an outdoor café in Paris, on a noisy corner of the Champs-Elysées. The boys were in an apartment around the corner, playing a video game on a laptop computer. David had agreed to watch his younger brothers while I slipped away for a quick walk. The early evening street was busy with stylishly dressed young Middle Eastern men, women in long black burkhas, and young Parisian women in tight jeans trailing cigarette smoke. The street was noisy and the lights blared. The twelve-dollar iced coffee that had just been placed in front of me was not iced at all but tepid and watery. I held my head in my hands. I was miserable.

What was I thinking? Whatever possessed me to bring three children to Paris?

I had always adored Paris. Paris was about romance and promise. It meant dreamy evenings sipping wine in cafés and walks along the Seine while a bright white moon rose in a black sky. Bill and I had spent a few intoxicating days here on our honeymoon—it was one of our best memories. Even on trips I had taken to Paris alone, such as the summer backpacking after college, I had spent happy, dreamy hours writing in a notebook at small, round tables surrounding the Place Saint-Michel, taken long walks through flower-bedecked public gardens, and delighted in seeing where the winding streets with their very Parisian blue and white street signs would take me. Paris was a place I didn't just enjoy—it was a place I inhaled. With or without wine, I always felt slightly drunk.

But this was an entirely different Paris. This Paris was about children's complaints. Complaints about TV shows that were useless because they were in French. About sandwiches made on oddly shaped bread and cheese with disgusting chalk crusts. This Paris generated complaints about boring monuments with nothing but old stuff and museums filled with "laminated pictures of ladies showing their private parts." Complaints about long, hot walks to get anywhere, down uninteresting streets. This Paris certainly wasn't about art or music or romance.

The trip had been planned for years. When I had decided to take my sons to see the solar eclipse, I had more than one motive. Besides wanting to share that once-in-a-lifetime experience with them, I had something to prove. I wanted my sons to see that just because their father wasn't around to plan travel itineraries in his exacting and capable way—not to mention to manage the heavy suitcases—it didn't mean we would never go anywhere again. This time, I would be the one bringing them a profound experience they would always remember.

Bill and I had been enthusiastic travelers, and when the locale wasn't too challenging or exotic, we often brought the children with us. Traveling with young children had required careful planning, but we managed well. Bill handled luggage, boarding passes, keys, driving, and unfamiliar public transportation. I packed, found local grocery stores, and supplied snacks, crayons, and puzzle books to keep the boys occupied while we waited for service in family-friendly restaurants. There were the usual tensions between the two of us. Bill always chided me for packing far more than we needed, while I clung to the security of always having more than enough of everything. I couldn't bear how strictly he kept us to a sightseeing schedule. One might think that lack of financial pressure—Bill's business was doing quite well in those years—would have lessened most conflicts between us caused by the stress of traveling, since we could afford any taxi ride or amenity to make life easier. This did not turn out to be the case. Bill and I managed to fight in the plushest of hotel suites.

This trip to Paris alone with my sons had not been easy so far. Now I was the only adult to take care of three children, both physically and financially. As the sole parent in charge, where there had once been two, I belatedly realized that the trip would be twice as much work. Add to this, I would have to handle it all in my clumsy, resurrected high school French.

After an exhausting overnight flight, an exorbitantly

expensive taxi ride from the airport to Paris already had me over budget. An apartment had been loaned to us by friends at home, so there would be no hotel cost. Circling the block off the Champs-Elysées with suitcases and three overtired boys in tow, searching for the store where the apartment keys had been left for us, I asked myself what insanity had possessed me to believe I could handle such an undertaking. I was to repeat this question to myself more than once over the next ten days.

The keys were in an envelope just where they were supposed to be, but at the apartment door, I still felt overwhelmed. Near tears, I strained to get the keys to open the ancient lock. Behind me the boys waited, jet-lagged and dirty, in the narrow hallway piled with our impossibly heavy luggage. I wished I hadn't packed so much.

David, although responsible about keeping an eye on his younger brothers or minding the luggage while I sought a taxi or some information, was a physically restless fourteen, given to provoking his brothers with cheerful nudges and pokes. Robert, twelve, was cooperative in a typical middle child way, but also easily bored and exhausted. For cranky six-year-old Alex, international travel was nothing but a highly bothersome inconvenience. ("They don't have *real* bread here," he said at our first meal, refusing the crusty baguette. "And this isn't real cheese—it's not square.")

Two days later, we made a brief visit to Napoleon's tomb. I had imagined that the sight of a coffin that held a real dead person would interest the boys, and it did—briefly. More interesting to Alex was the machine with the big crank, which, for an additional five franc deposit, pressed a deposited coin into a large commemorative medallion bearing Napoleon's likeness on one side and his coffin on the other. Alex had insisted on one, most likely, I imagined, so he could turn the crank.

It was a hot afternoon when we left Napoleon's tomb. I insisted we stop afterward at the nearby Hôtel des Invalides, a massive monument-like building with a huge courtyard. Originally built as a hospital for war veterans, it now housed a military museum with antique rifles and cannons that I believed might hold the boys' interest, but did so only briefly.

On our way back to the apartment—to do what, I had no idea, but clearly we were all out of steam—we headed down the long avenue in front of the monument. Alongside the sidewalk was a low stone wall, and on the other side of the wall, a deep, grass-filled moat that had once protected the Hôtel des Invalides from invaders. I was tired, hot, and growing increasingly exasperated at having to stop whenever Alex tossed his commemorative franc into the air and tried to catch it. "Alex, stop doing that, it's going to roll into the street, and I don't want you running out to get it," I said to deaf ears. Rather than help keep him in line, his older brothers were encouraging him in his coin toss. I was at my wit's end. On the other hand, this seemed to be the most interest Alex had shown in anything on what was clearly to him a tedious, annoying vacation.

Alex stopped one more time. "I'm going to catch it this time, watch," he said.

I sighed, and we all stopped. Alex tossed the franc high

overhead. It made a graceful arc, not toward the street, but in the direction of the Hôtel des Invalides. Then it was gone—simply disappeared. Alex looked around, dumbfounded.

Robert raced over to the side of the wall alongside the moat. "There it is!" he shouted. There was Alex's franc, six feet down, nestled in the grassy floor of the moat.

The absurdity of Alex having tossed his valuable new souvenir into the moat took hold of us, and we all started to laugh. Even Alex, fighting back frustrated tears, couldn't help himself from laughing. We flopped down on the sidewalk and gave in to the silliness of it.

It occurred to me that this was the first time on this trip that anyone seemed to be having a good time. Which immediately got me wondering: Could this moment only have happened on an arduous, expensive trip to Paris? If Alex had accidentally tossed a quarter onto the subway tracks from the Seventh Avenue IRT platform in New York City, just a short distance from our home, wouldn't we have enjoyed the moment just as much?

And then another thought. When was the last time I had laughed with my sons this way? And had I ever? The question was a revelation.

I don't know exactly when I had begun to sense I was losing the affection of my three little boys. When they were infants, I didn't question how important I was in their lives. But even then their father had readily taken over a good many bonding moments, like shoulder carries and bath time. When they became toddlers, reading at bedtime had become his purview as well. Always conscious of how my brothers had grown up basically fatherless, I was thrilled that my sons had a loving, involved father. I encouraged it in every way possible—leaving out clean pajamas in the next room while he played with them in the bath, listening while he gently shampooed their hair in the special way that kept the soap out of their eyes. As they grew, more and more it began to feel to me like Bill had become the loving parent, while I felt like . . . what? The drone.

One day, not long after the birth of our third son, the five of us were in the car. Seven-year-old David had secured the coveted front seat next to his dad. Rob and I were in the back with Alex in the infant seat between us. "I have an idea, Dad," said David, who had become a Nickelodeon fan. "Now that we have three boys in this family, you and Mom can get divorced. Then you can marry a woman who has three girls. Then we can be like the Brady Bunch."

"But what about me?" I said from the backseat. "I'd miss you if I wasn't part of this family any more."

David thought about this for a moment. "Okay, Mom. You could be the maid."

Bill and I laughed. It seemed funny at the time. But for some reason the words kept coming back to me. In time the memory would no longer make me laugh.

Years later, I sat across the ebony desk of a divorce attorney. The first thing we would discuss were custody issues. Bill was by then passionately close to his sons. Besides still taking responsibility for baths, stories, and long talks at bedtime, Bill always found time to take them for weekend rides in his vintage pickup truck or to Cub Scout meetings. On vacations it was always their father alongside them on amusement park rides or playing miniature golf, while I held jackets or tended to a baby. At home, I was usually far too busy to play board games with the boys, and video games didn't interest me. As the boys grew older, I felt more and more excluded from this male-only club. I began to feel lonely in my own family.

Facing the attorney, I was terrified of what might happen now that we were separating. Bill was the good parent—the loved one, the fun one. I was the one who always seemed in a hurry or spoke sharply when I lost patience. Bill was gentle and forgiving with the boys at all times. I was fearful that if asked to choose, the boys would want to live with their father. Would it come to that?

The lawyer held his pen over a yellow pad. "When it comes to custody decisions, the court always considers the degree of each parent's prior involvement with the children. Let me ask you a few questions. Which of you schedules pediatrician visits and takes them to appointments?"

"I do, of course," I answered.

"What about play dates with other children?" I did that, too.

"Buys them their clothes? Shoes? Vitamins?" Yes, also me.

"I want you to make two lists and bring them to me next time we meet," said the lawyer. "On one page I want you to list all the items you do related to the children—every last thing—everything you arrange or buy or do for them. On the other list, write down all the things your husband does for them."

I started on my list on the train home that afternoon. One page quickly filled, followed by another. First came the major responsibilities, which I admitted were mine: researching preschools and then enrolling them; furnishing their rooms; planning and preparing meals; scheduling pediatric appointments for checkups, immunizations, and illnesses. These were followed by the less obvious: planning birthday parties; buying school supplies; signing them up for swim lessons, gymnastics, and art programs; keeping their toys organized and battery-stocked; monitoring and replacing outgrown clothes; packing backpacks. Then I got down to a staggering amount of minutiae: clipping fingernails; sewing on Boy Scout patches; buying gifts for other children's birthday parties; filling out permission slips and absence notes; taking them for haircuts.

By the third page, I was flabbergasted by the volume of work that caring for three children entailed. I had never stopped to look at it that way.

Then I began the list of my husband's responsibilities. Baths. Putting them to bed with bedtime stories. Boy Scouts. The fun stuff. Oh, yes, and he attended Open School nights and parent teacher conferences.

There were four items on his list. There had to be more, I thought. He was the real parent, wasn't he? But that was it. Four items, to my seventy-nine.

I held the lists up side by side and began to cry. Until that moment, I hadn't really been sure that I was all that important to my sons.

Our divorce agreement eventually called for joint custody. The children's primary residence was defined as with me, which Bill never challenged. During the time that the children were at home with me, which was most of the week and every other weekend, I tried to keep our home life as unchanged as possible from our orderly two-parent household. But a lot of things were different than before. Instead of dinnertime occurring promptly at six, which Bill had insisted on so the children wouldn't get too hungry, the arrival of our evening meal was a moving target that could creep toward seven or even seven thirty. This would sometimes require me to run upstairs to the boys with a plate filled with cucumbers cut into swords and an apologetic "Dinner's coming soon, guys . . . I promise." The boys hardly seemed to notice the delay; in fact, they seemed perfectly content to watch more of *The Simpsons* as they reached for their appetizer.

But nothing after the divorce changed quite as much as family vacations. Initially, I insisted on planning one or two of these a year. My rationale was that it was important to do this to keep my sons' lives as consistent as they had been before the divorce. But there was something competitive about my motive as well. Bill was taking the boys on one exciting and expensive adventure after another during his planned vacations with them—ski trips to Canada and Aspen, a dude ranch out West, a trip to Barcelona, Spain. One summer he took them to a baseball game at every Major League stadium in California. My old insecurities resurfaced. If the boys were having so much fun on these trips with their father, would they come to love him more? Would it be the same as before, when "Dad" meant fun and travel, and "Mom" meant "Please put your plates in the dishwasher" and "You're due for a haircut"? And why shouldn't I take my children on those exotic, high-priced vacation adventures that Bill was so clearly enjoying with them?

Two attempts at trying to outdo their father at vacations gave me my answer, which unfortunately I was to learn the hard way. First there was a misguided ski weekend when I discovered that it is physically impossible for one mother to keep track of four sets of skis, poles, and boots, in addition to the usual hats, gloves, turtle furs, and snacks. Then came that exhausting and unappreciated trip to Paris. Besides which, on my own now financially, I simply could no longer afford it. The far-too expensive trip to Paris would be my last attempt at international family travel. Even trips to visit my mother in Orlando, Florida, where there was no need for a hotel, became too expensive when plane flights and theme park admission tickets were included.

Eventually I had to face the fact that where vacations were concerned, I would have to scale down my ambitions.

That next year, when planning our summer vacation, I thought about the New Jersey shore, which was only a three-hour drive away. I still held wonderful memories of the New Jersey beach and boardwalk towns from my annual summertime visits to my father. It was loud and commercial, certainly nowhere that Bill would have found appealing. The beaches were crowded, to be sure; but the Atlantic Ocean was icy and clean and the waves the best there were. Even better, most beaches had lifeguards, so I might actually be able to relax while the boys rode their boogie boards. Maybe we could go to Atlantic City. At least one night each summer I had been able to cajole my father into taking us there. In my memory it was a magic fairyland where I had been dazzled by the lights, frozen custard, and exotic pedicycles on the boardwalk.

A call to the Atlantic City Visitors Bureau changed my mind. "Don't take your kids here," said the woman on the phone. "There's not much other than gambling here, and they won't be able to get in anywhere because they're underage. You might try Ocean City instead."

Only twelve miles north, Ocean City was a dry town, she explained—no alcohol, which made it a family vacation spot, not popular with partying types. "Besides the beach, there's a boardwalk with a lot of things for kids to do. They'll have a better time." So Ocean City it was.

Being late in the season, all I could get was a long weekend's reservation for one large but very cramped room that the hotel promised could be made to sleep four. Along with a fold-out double sofa and a cot supplied by the hotel for an extra ten dollars per day, there would be a pullout chair that offered an additional single bed. Most important, it had an alcove mini-kitchen where I could assemble simple breakfasts and picnic lunches for the beach, which would save on restaurant meals. We would make do. I didn't much enjoy taking my sons to restaurants, anyway. Now in their early teens, David and Robert were constantly emitting pent-up energy, with arms, elbows, and knees in constant motion. Eight-year-old Alex, always eager to please his older brothers, would giggle and egg them on. Inevitably the three boys would usually end up jostling, poking, and carousing as I grew more impatient and frustrated waiting for service.

At my first glimpse at the Ocean City boardwalk, the

scene was so ugly that my eyes hurt. Screaming signs for amusement rides, video arcades, miniature golf, pizza, salt water taffy, virtual reality rides, and souvenir stands competed for airspace. The Boardwalk teemed with families bulging out of shorts and T-shirts, with midriffs jiggling as they ate huge frozen custard cones and powdered sugar–dusted fried dough.

Squinting, I surveyed the scene. It was a far cry from the beach resort in Sanibel, Florida, where Bill and I had last taken the boys when we were still married. But no matter, we were here. The ocean was still the ocean, although it was hard to glimpse much seawater in between the bodies that crowded the areas between the green flags that marked where the lifeguards permitted swimmers. Inside the hotel I was relieved to note that the boys, older and stronger now, were a big help with the suitcases and grocery bags. Within a few minutes of checking in, we were in our room.

It was all there—the sofa, the cot, the tiny kitchenette. But as soon as our luggage was deposited on the floor, we were cramped for floor space. "Is there room for all of us in here, Mom?" asked David, looking dubious. "I only see places for three people to sleep."

Robert had already figured out how to remove cushions off a small slipper chair and was tossing them aside. He unfolded a diminutive mattress. "Look, it's a wiener bed!" he cried.

"Shotgun I don't get the wiener bed!" David called out.

"Shotgun I don't get the wiener bed!" said Robert.

"Alex gets the wiener bed!" said David, flopping on the sofa.

"How come I get the wiener bed?" said Alex.

"'Cause you're the wiener, Alex!" said Rob and David, in unison.

I had set down my suitcase to laugh at these three wonderful, ridiculous goofy guys.

For the rest of our stay in Ocean City all someone had to say were the words *wiener bed* to send everyone into laughing fits. It seemed that we laughed every minute for the next four days. If someone got rowdy at dinner, all I had to do was say "Behave, or you'll get the wiener bed," and the boys would be falling off their chairs with silly laughter. More than once, water went up someone's nose.

On the boardwalk, the boys were ecstatic. It was video game heaven. Three days would hardly be enough to try out every arcade and amusement. "This is the coolest place you've ever taken us, Mom," said Robert, his voice raised above the blare of carousel music and screams from a roller coaster.

The boys decided that their first activity would be that amazing double-decker pirate-themed miniature golf game right next to the hotel. I handed Robert money for the three of them, with instructions to come back to our room directly afterward for an early dinner. I would be in the room unpacking.

"Aren't you going play with us, Mom?" said David.

"Yeah, Mom, you come, too," said Rob. "Come on, four people makes a perfect tournament."

It hadn't occurred to me. I hadn't played miniature golf since I was a child. And in all my married years vacationing with the children, their father made up the foursome, not me. I was surprised to be asked.

"I don't think I'd be very good," I answered. "I'll just slow you down."

"Ah, come on, Mom! We'll teach you," said Rob.

So for the first time ever, I played a game of miniature golf with my three sons. It was an entirely new experience. By the end of eighteen holes, I discovered something new about each of my children whom I had believed I knew so well. I learned David, with the confidence of a firstborn, seemed to slip naturally into a leadership role with his brothers, while being gracious and agreeable when one of them objected to his decisions. Robert had a surprisingly dry wit for a twelve-year-old and kept me laughing with his asides about my athletic prowess or lack thereof. Alex turned out to be particularly skilled with a golf club and easily beat me and both of his older brothers. I discovered that I wasn't so bad at it myself and got fully into the fun of the game. When I made a hole-in-one at the Dark Dungeon eighth hole, I stopped to do a hip-twitching victory dance at the tee, fingers pointed skyward, while the boys applauded me with "Way to go, Mom!" and Alex, embarrassed, looked around to make sure no one else noticed.

I felt several years younger and lighter as I stood at the admission window paying for a second game. And to think I might have missed this.

Later that night, as the boys watched Nickelodeon on the pullout sofa and I read on the cot, I thought back on the years Bill and I had vacationed with the children. Why had I so readily relinquished the role of the fun parent to Bill? Why was I the one to absent myself, to read on the beach or wander the shops, while he did the fun things?

My obvious rationale was that Bill was, after all, that natural leader of this boys-only club. I just assumed the boys would rather be in a male presence than to be with their mother. But I remembered something more. Whenever I allowed myself to be part of the otherwise male-only group of Bill and his sons, I had been uncomfortable. There was the usual marriage tension between Bill and me, as he and I rarely agreed on anything. In addition, I was insecure about my own mothering style under Bill's critical and protective-of-his-sons eyes. Lose patience, speak to anyone sharply, keep everyone waiting to stop at a restroom or to run back to the hotel room for one more thing, suggest a variation from Bill's carefully arranged itinerary, or, God help me, utter a four-letter word in front of the children when a plate of ketchup-laden French fries was elbowed onto my lap— any of these would elicit Bill's opprobrium, silent or otherwise.

No one had excluded me from this family. I had excluded myself. I had removed myself not only because it seemed to be a closed, all-male group but also because I was uncomfortable in the marriage. But now I was free to be whoever I was with my children. Maybe they would hear an occasional expletive or two. So, they'd discover how imperfect and human their mother was. I was sure they'd survive.

But would they love me anyway?

Those four days in Ocean City were the most fun I had ever had on any vacation, either with or without the children. I discovered that if being a single parent meant twice as much work, it also meant four times as much fun. Filling a car of our own on the huge Ferris wheel, the four of us sat so close that our knees bumped together and Robert leaned against me as the car swung high above the amusement park. I was actually surprised by how anxious the boys were to have me accompany them on the rides—"Come on, Mom, you could do the bumper cars, they're really not scary, I promise!" Nevertheless, I was glad to have underaged Alex as my excuse to skip the roller coaster and go with him instead to the frozen custard stand.

The following year we returned to Ocean City for a full week's vacation. This time I planned ahead and was able to rent a much roomier one-bedroom condo with a well-outfitted kitchen. Although we would once again avoid restaurants, and I had prepaid for the condo, I realized that a week's worth of video games and amusement park rides could become a very expensive undertaking. I would have to keep careful watch on our expenses. But I worried that my sons, accustomed to what probably felt like their father's unlimited resources, might feel deprived when they were with me. Would they resent my penuriousness? Again, a sense of competition with Bill's financial prowess rose up.

I came up with an idea. I brought with me seven fifty-dollar bills, one for each day of our stay.

The first morning I handed the boys a fifty dollar bill. I could tell that they were impressed by the large amount, and the crisp bill's unfamiliar denomination. "I'm going to give you one of these every morning. Each day, it is to be divided exactly by three," I told them. "Each of you has complete discretion to spend your share on anything you want—any miniature golf game, amusement park ride, entertainment, or souvenir. I'll be paying for all meals—if you want a sandwich for lunch, I'll make it for you back here. But if you want to buy any restaurant food or snacks, it comes from this as well. Whatever you don't spend, you get to keep when you go home."

The boys couldn't believe my largesse. Fifty dollars a day! It was the most money that had ever been placed directly in their hands. They quickly figured out it would work out to just under seventeen dollars for each of them. It still seemed a huge amount of money. Whereas my first instinct would have been to hand the bill to David every day by right of his being the oldest, I decided to let the younger ones know I deemed them trustworthy as well. So each day a different boy—even Alex, the youngest— took his turn receiving and breaking the fifty dollar bill. Then, immediately after breakfast each morning they were off to boardwalk heaven. Afternoons would be spent on the beach.

On the first day the boys realized that a ten-dollar movie admission, along with Robert's additional six dollars for a soda and snack, took up far too much of their entire day's allotment. "Too expensive," said David. "Can't we just rent movies instead? Maybe there's a Blockbuster around here." Indeed there was one just a few blocks away, and I was happy to ante up the three-dollar video rental fee for a movie in our condo each night.

The boys had so much fun that week, they barely realized they had been given a surreptitious lesson in finance. They carefully planned and budgeted each day's activities so that by week's end, they had hit all the highlights. They quickly learned which rides were total rip-offs, which video arcades produced the most bonus games, and that the boardwalk pizza was both soggy and overpriced. There was some borrowing and lending back and forth, but the transactions were honorable and good-natured. No one bought a souvenir all week.

In the years since my divorce, freed from the tension and uneasiness of a difficult marriage, I have been able to develop a relationship with my sons I had never really known. For better or worse, I let them see who I was, with all my flaws. They are unfazed by my impatience and meltdowns, my forgetfulness, and even my occasional four-letter word. I watch my boys stand a little taller as I let them know that I depend on them—that I look to their strengths to make up for my own weaknesses, whether it is to steady me in tense situations ("Calm down, Mom," is all Robert has to gently say to me, hand on my shoulder, to diffuse an impending eruption) or, once they sprouted into teens, to reach for a jar on a high shelf.

I'm not perfect, and I make many parenting mistakes. When the boys became teenagers, they found plenty to disagree with me about. But I told them that I was always ready to hear and consider their grievances. We speak to each other with affection and respect. The boys still laugh at me and roll their eyes at the ridiculous things I do and say, like telling them to put their napkins on their lap at dinner ("What for? Didn't you just finish telling us 'This isn't a restaurant'?"). They recount and make fun of "Mom" stories, like the time I tried to drive and read a Florida map at the same time and ended up putting seven hundred dollars in damage to Grandma's car. But there is never sarcasm or derision. Only patient, long-suffering love.

In all the years I had felt trapped in my marriage, one overwhelming fear, more than any other, kept me imprisoned. It was the fear that should we divorce, my sons might lose their father. What I discovered instead was that through the divorce, my sons gained a mother—the mother they might never have had.

What I gained, I cannot even begin to measure.

Service Contract

As a fairly recent new homeowner, I'd love to profess that being required to learn a whole new set of home maintenance skills filled me with newfound pride and pleasure. But it's just not so. Much as I reject the suggestion that household jobs should be assigned along gender lines, I'm forced to admit that I'd much rather marinate a piece of swordfish in ginger-teriyaki broth than replace my hall closet's wobbly old doorknob, even though the daily satisfaction of seeing a shiny, newly installed brass knob that shuts with a reassuring click will last long after that perfectly grilled swordfish is obliterated from both existence and memory.

Sure, I'm proud of my house. And I'll move heaven and earth to keep it in good repair. But I've given up pretending to like all that home maintenance entails—or to be very good at it.

When I became the lone adult responsible for our

home, I was soon plunged into the world of home maintenance. In the early years I resolved to learn how to handle all those tasks my former husband once tackled. After all, what could be so difficult? In an "I Am Woman, Hear Me Roar" mood, I set out for Home Depot where I bought myself not one toolbox, but two: a shiny fire-engine red one for hammer, screwdrivers, pliers, and the like; and a bright yellow plastic box for screws, picture hooks, and nails, which I kept nestled in neat compartments like the spools of thread in my sewing box.

Then came the tools. I had voiced no objections when Bill took his tools with him when we separated; I had taken my kitchen utensils. This would be an opportunity to hand select new ones of my own. Bill had once mentioned that Sears Craftsman tools carried a lifetime guarantee, so Sears Craftsmen it would be. I resolved to keep my toolboxes neat—nothing like Bill's rusty, jumbled mess.

Over that first year of home ownership, as I took on what should have been modest little projects, I became humbly acquainted with my limitations in the home maintenance department. I installed window blinds in the bedrooms that raise to a permanent tilt. I built a prefabricated "Some Assembly Required" stereo cabinet that several weeks after assembly split apart at the joints, scattering CDs all over the floor. Finally, when I smashed a decorative ceiling globe while trying to change one single, stupid lightbulb, I gave up.

Today, my toolboxes are such a jumble I would be hard-pressed to locate a retractable razor to scrape off last year's beach sticker, let alone a proper tool.

Nevertheless, I've achieved a peaceful level of acceptance regarding my home maintenance ineptitude. What I've discovered instead is that there is a world of men out there—okay, let's call a spade a spade, they *are* usually always male—who love nothing more than to take on home repair challenges while imparting their expertise to the ignorant. I don't like to play the "helpless female card," but I am female. And I am, let's face it, pretty helpless when it comes to things like my furnace.

I've learned that the most beautiful words in the English language are not *I love you;* they're *I have a service contract.* I use those magic words to summon my knights in oily armor—the oil company emergency night crew—when there is a hissing spray shooting out of the hot water heater, say, or the furnace fails to kick on during a particularly frigid night. The service guys can usually diagnose the cause of my furnace emergency in about twelve seconds and fix it in less than nine minutes. But they then spend the next forty-five minutes attempting to educate me on the intricacies of my home's hot water and heating systems, with an analysis of what went wrong and why. Many a frigid winter night (including one New Year's Eve when my oil tanks ran completely dry) I have shivered in a parka wrapped over my nightgown while they earnestly explained whatever it was *this time* that put the furnace in hibernation or made the hot water disappear. Like it or not, I get the full rundown. "This is the pressure relief valve." "This switch trips the reset." "Here's where the hot water line from the boiler (*boiler* being another word for furnace, which it took me about two years to figure out) hooks up with the main

water intake." But five minutes after they've solved whatever crisis brought my home to the brink of disaster, the
lesson is gone from my mind, and by the next morning
has completely dissipated as snow above my poorly insu-
lated roof.

Then there are those men of a certain age—retired, I
imagine, but with fix-it skills just begging to be put to
use—who work in my neighborhood hardware stores.
Finding me wandering the aisles dazed, they pounce with
words that are music to this middle-aged mother: "What
can I do for you, young lady?" They freely dole out advice:
"You don't want this wood glue; it dries yellow. Use this
one. You're going to need a molly for that wood screw, or
it's not going to hold. Three-quarter inch should do it.
And make sure you screw into a stud," they warn. (This
last admonishment is offered with such solemnity that I've
never gotten up the courage to ask: "But what if I don't
want to hang the picture where the stud is?") These elderly gentleman flex their home maintenance skills with no
less dedication than muscle men on Venice beach.

I breathe a great sigh of relief knowing that out there,
in addition to the oil company night emergency crew and
the hardware store gurus, are the electricians, plumbers,
appliance servicemen, exterminators, and emergency
drain cleaners who have rescued me again and again. I
even have an all-around handyman named Rich, also a
retired guy, who drives through town in a truck with the
words Handy Hubby painted on the side and will come
every season to replace the screens with storm windows,
install the window air conditioners, and fix my kitchen
cabinets when they cave in.

Oh, yes—and he did a really good job putting a new brass knob on my closet door. It brings me the greatest satisfaction every time I turn it.

My Lost Romance.com

As luck would have it I became single just about the time that online dating made an appearance. Divorced in my early forties and with three young sons, I hadn't dated in over two decades and didn't have the slightest clue how or where to begin. But here was this amazingly simple, risk-free solution. Out there, somewhere, was the perfect man. All I had to do was log on and find him.

Maybe because there was a cyber-age coolness to it, online dating seemed to carry none of the "Dear Miss Lonely Hearts" stigma of the singles ads that became popular some years back but to which few people admitted resorting. Or maybe online dating had more prestige because its "getting acquainted" stage by e-mail required a certain level of literacy. I was pleasantly surprised to find, after signing on to my first one-week trial membership in a popular online dating site, that the site seemed populated by a large number of highly respectable, perfectly reasonable single men. I discovered the further good news that fatherhood is now quite different than it was decades ago when divorced men instantly relocated to the city after leaving their wives in the suburbs to raise the kids. Instead, there were now a great many men committed to staying close to their children, right here in my own and nearby towns. And a wealth of them were cruising profiles on Match.com.

It was a brave, new world, I thought. This was going to be easy.

But online dating, I was to discover quite quickly, carried its own brave, new dangers. Sifting quickly through the scores of men whose profiles said that their idea of a perfect date was "holding hands while walking on the beach" (so common was this, one wonders why the beaches are not a lot more crowded at sunset with hand-holding middle-aged pairs), I hit the jackpot.

In my inbox, one night, appeared someone I will call Paul. He was a classical music and opera lover with whom I quickly began exchanging lengthy e-mails about the relative merits of *Turandot* versus *Otello,* Jean-Yves Thibaudet's opera transcriptions, and the Swedish tenor Jussi Björling (we both considered him our all-time favorite opera singer). Without being bothered by shallow and unimportant details such as the man's physical appearance, mannerisms, or financial status—I was far too spiritually evolved to care about those—I indulged in a long, rapturous e-mail correspondence (I'm a writer, remember) spanning several weeks. Fairly soon a fantasy man of my dreams began to take shape. Along with the "brown eyes, thinning brown hair" supplied in Paul's first e-mail, I envisioned someone tall and brawny, but in a softened, early-fifties Harrison Ford kind of way.

Our e-mail conversations were captivating and soon took up my entire evenings after I put the boys to bed. In rapid-fire exchanges that sometimes ran into late nights, this well-educated, articulate, classical music–loving man and I got to know each other. What a marvel this e-mail dating was! Here I was, getting to know the heart and soul of a man, through our words and thoughts alone. I was able to share my inner self, without the utterly stupid distractions of physical appearance, dress, and all the other shallow, outward manifestations of financial success. Who cared what kind of car he drove or whether he worked out at a gym? He wrote that he had a Ph.D. in biochemistry and taught at a prestigious university nearby. Ah! A man of music *and* science! That was good enough for me.

But even better was the chance to present a carefully crafted image of myself in a completely new and unrestrained way. This called for creativity—and of that, I had plenty. Calling upon all my literary and writer's skills, I went to work intellectually seducing this man with my articulate musings on the many moods of Dvorak. I wrote of how Mendelssohn's musical development from his earliest symphonies was a perfect replication of his maturing view of the world. I mused about how listening to Björling's *Pearl Fishers* duet made me fall in love a little bit, each time. In turn he introduced me to his particular passion, Mahler's Third Symphony. He convinced me to appreciate Wagner—even the long boring parts.

That he prized Mahler and, by God, Wagner, sealed it for me. Here was a man's man! I was in love. What a wonder this Internet dating turned out to be! How it transformed what I remembered of my mother's post-divorce 1960s and 1970s dating life, with those dismal Parents-Without-Partners dances from which she often came home depressed. It was truly a wonderful new world. My single days were clearly numbered.

During that full month of impassioned, late night e-mailing, there wasn't the slightest hint of sex. Of course not. This was about the soul, not the body. We were both too committed to expressing thoughts, ideas, feelings, and aesthetic sensibilities to even approach the corpo-real. Not yet, anyway, I thought. But a palpable under-tone of romance lingered.

Finally, one brave moment on a sultry summer evening, I suggested we meet. I was jumping out of my skin and could wait no longer. We scheduled a phone call for the next evening. In my room with the door closed, I lit candles by the phone, turned down the light.

He called on schedule. Paul's voice, "Oh my Gawd, I can't believe how wonderful it has been corresponding with you this way!"—a gush, actually—had a high-pitched, feminine twang with a heavy overlay of Queens, New York. I could barely manage a few choked words—my articulate thoughts and endless flood of words had come to a complete stop. The more Paul spoke, the worse it got. This was nothing like what my Harrison Ford version of Paul was supposed to sound like. He was practically lisping, for God's sake. Stammering and near speechless, I hurried off the phone but agreed to meet him for lunch later in the week.

By the end of the phone call I knew that Paul—the Paul of my imagination, the big guy, the man's man—was dead. I could see him so well—the frizzled, brown and thinning hair, the big chest that still looked good in decade-old tennis shirts, the kind face with the soft brown eyes. And he was dead—I had lost him!

For two days I couldn't shake my mournful mood. I wallowed in the idea that I was like Cyrano's poor Rosalind. I, too, had loved and lost my own Cyrano—but without the benefit of even having met him. All the while I sensed the humor in the situation, knowing that I had brought this on myself with my wild imagination. No one, in fact, had actually died. But that didn't help.

Several days later the real Paul stepped out of his sports car in my driveway. He was a lovely, elderly, well-dressed gentleman with a slight build and impeccable manners. He wore patent leather Guccis with bare ankles and a red silk handkerchief tucked into the pocket of his perfectly pressed seersucker suit. By the time we met, with a two-day mourning period behind me, my mood had lifted a bit, and I had returned to reality. I greeted Paul cordially at the door. Perhaps this man's hair had at one time been brown, but if so, there was no evidence of it in the bits of gray that encircled a nearly bald head. By now I was fully prepared for the nasal, high-pitched lilt in Paul's voice.

Driving to a country inn for lunch, Paul filled me in on his passion for Louis Quinze antique furniture (pronouncing it "caaans" with a flat New York "a"), which, unfortunately, had gone to his ex-wife in the divorce. I had to wonder whether his ex-wife seemed to have suspected the same thing about Paul that I had. And whether Paul himself would be the last to know. No matter. By then my other Paul—the Harrison Ford Paul—had faded into romantic nostalgia, while the Louis Quinze Paul with perfectly knotted silk tie and natty suit treated me to a pleasant springtime lunch on a flower-bedecked veranda.

I didn't give up entirely on Internet dating after that, but adopted a strict rule. After one e-mail, we talk on the phone. Two e-mails, we meet for coffee. Nonnegotiable. I direct my creative writing energies elsewhere. And rarely, if ever, listen to Mahler.

First Dates . . . and Other Comedies

O nly a few months after Bill and I let the world know that we were officially separated, I was pleasantly surprised by a phone call. A woman from our temple called to ask whether I would be interested in dating a recently divorced single friend of hers. "He's a doctor, successful, and quite wealthy," she said. "A full head of hair, a little shy. A nice guy, very intelligent."

Wow, this was easy, I thought. After all the horror stories about how single women outnumber available men a gazillion-to-one, I had been fully expecting to go years before finding someone to date. And a doctor, no less. Not that I was all that interested in dating yet. I was still thoroughly enjoying the peace and serenity that came after years of discord and not feeling the least bit in need of a new romantic partner. But the idea of getting dressed up and being taken to dinner was a welcome one.

However, I worried, too. It would be my first date after

my separation and a blind date at that. Was I attractive enough to go out on a date? I was far from slender in those Ben & Jerry's–enriched months following my divorce. Would he be disappointed when we met?

I realized quite quickly upon meeting him that my friend had deliberately selected the *full head of hair* description to avoid other terms such as *overweight* and *striking resemblance to a bulldog*. But no matter. I had come way too far to judge a person on looks, I reminded myself.

Our conversation was pleasant enough, centering on our careers, classical music, his grown children. What he was most interested in talking about was his collection of antique watches. *Aha! This is good, I have discovered his passion* was my first thought—but things quickly went downhill. Although I consider myself a fairly good conversationalist, I found it difficult to pretend to find antique watches interesting, or come up with a single intelligent question other than why one would want to wear an old, inaccurate watch when the twenty dollar quartz battery-powered Casio versions worked so flawlessly. He told me about his new apartment in the city, trips to Hilton Head, and how he had recently been promoted to chief of staff of his specialty at a prestigious teaching hospital.

Fairly soon the conversation turned to our divorces. Being single had left him with a lot of time to spend on launching a new research division, not to mention golf. Remembering the "quite wealthy" reference—or perhaps thinking of my own situation—I couldn't keep my thoughts from turning to his ex-wife. "And how did she come out of the divorce?" I asked, with compassion. "Is your ex-wife all right?"

"Is she all right? Are you kidding? She's a pig in shit," he answered. And then he actually snorted.

Now that was attractive. After a kind "no, thank you" after his request in the parking lot for a second date, I had a good laugh most of the way home at this inauspicious—or auspicious, I wasn't sure which—introduction to postdivorce dating.

Beginning with what I'll always think fondly of as my "Pig in Shit" first date, dating thereafter continued to be one long life lesson that what one worries about never turns out to have been worth worrying about at all. The corollary to this, of course, is that the things you don't anticipate are the ones that are going to rise up and kick you in the butt.

Such it was with all my preconceived dating worries. I fretted: *Who will be interested in a woman with three children? Will my young sons be psychologically damaged seeing me with any man other than their father? And if it does develop into more than just dating, what about AIDS?—my God, I haven't been on the other end of a condom since I was a teenager. Will men find me a dud because I don't drink?*

I had yet to realize that a far greater worry should have been the opposite, which was this: how could I possibly find anyone attractive, now that I didn't drink? Having a drink with a blind date when the drink consisted of a club soda with lime resulted in what I came to call the "What You See Is What You Got" Effect. Without the happy, edge-softening buzz provided by alcohol, no man ever looked any more attractive or interesting than he actually was. Although this made for a great many dull evenings, I later came to see this as a very good thing. Let's just say the condom thing never came up.

Unlike many newly divorced people, I had not started out dreading the thought of dating. During the later years of my ailing marriage I had more than a few silent fantasies about what it might be like to start anew. Although I soon discovered that they were indeed fantasies, the reality of dating turned out to be nothing at all like the horror stories I imagined. I learned that with the right attitude, a full reservoir of humor, genuine interest in other human beings, and a "what have I got to lose?" approach to any new encounter, dating became, like my solo travels, just one more interesting adventure.

I discovered quite quickly that I was a near-neophyte when it came to dating. I had married young, and in my previous 1970s college and grad school years there had been no such thing as dating, per se. I had acquired my first boyfriend hanging out in the open-door rooms of our freshman coed dorm. This was followed by a passionate eighteen-month long relationship with the junior (my first upperclassman) who had organized the group trip to Puerto Rico over winter break. Again there was no dating, only a lot of poolside and airport flirting to launch that romance. No one called me for a date back then. One minute I was in someone's black-lighted fraternity bedroom listening to the Moody Blues, and the next thing I knew, I was having regular Sunday tofu-and-egg breakfasts at the Moosewood Restaurant with a new boyfriend.

But skip ahead a few decades and there I was, in my

forties, single and a mother of three, facing the prospect of real dates for the first time. The warnings about "what's out there" began to roll in from other divorced women supposedly being helpful. It would be impossible to meet single men in the suburbs, I was advised. ("Once they dump their wives they all head out to the city.") With complete authority I was informed that there were fifty single women for each available man, and further-more, it was a damn good chance that that one available man would be looking for a younger woman. Should I be fortunate enough to chance upon a yet-unmarried man (read: unencumbered with ex-wife and children), he would certainly be looking for someone young and fer-tile with whom to start a new family. This ruled me out entirely, with my childbearing years well behind me, and three growing sons in tow.

The "It's impossible to meet men in the suburbs" warning was the first to tumble. There were the infre-quent, well-intentioned fix-up phone calls from women in the temple (who were a veritable gushing fountain of fix-up calls to recently divorced men like Bill, I later learned). There was online dating, although this had the potential to eat up a great many evening hours with min-imal payoff. And then there were the over-forty singles parties.

Although it would have been far more accurate to call many of these "over-sixty" parties, these were often dances organized by profiteers who charged an arm and a leg to attend a party in a restaurant lounge where the exorbitantly priced drinks cost an additional limb. Such evenings were perhaps the hardest to get geared up for.

Unlike the all-soul, no-body introductions in online dating, I knew from the outset that whether one was
approached at these parties, either male or female, would
be *strictly* about how one looked. I didn't think I looked
too bad, but I had born three children, after all. I also
dressed fairly conservatively, even for a singles event,
where low-cut cocktail dresses intended to display maximum cleavage seemed to be de rigueur. These had never
exactly been my style, particularly due to my failure to
meet the basic requirement of having some cleavage to
display.

I learned to mentally psyche myself up for these potentially ego-battering bouts. There were two components
to this approach, I discovered. First, I had to strictly banish any wistful and self-indulgent "Will I ever be loved
again?" thoughts. Second, comfortable shoes were
required. After standing in line to pay a pricey entrance
fee, I would turn in my drink ticket for my club soda,
then join the passing parade, a steady two-way stream of
opposing lanes that formed in the room (which I came to
think of as the pageant runway), with middle-aged singles furtively giving each other the once- and twice-over
while trying to look casual about it. I kept the mental pep
talk streaming in my head constantly. *How I or anyone else
looks isn't important,* I told myself. *This isn't just about finding someone to date. Look for the positive. If nothing else, here in
the suburbs where it feels like the entire world is either paired up
or married, isn't it good simply to be here to remind myself that
I'm not the only unmarried person in the entire state?*

Another approach was to call upon my journalist
training and strike up ad hoc interviews with men—and

not infrequently with women as well—to learn about their businesses or how they found their way into their careers. I challenged myself to learn one new fact about the world from every conversation—and unless someone was making a quick getaway after looking me over, many discoveries were really quite fascinating. I learned about a major coffee importing business in the next town over. I heard from an economist the prevailing theory about the effect of the labor shortage on the state's fiscal health, which I used the following week in an article I was writing for a local business journal. From a retired barber I learned that there is in this world one career that is guaranteed, 100 percent recession-proof. "No matter what happens, hair grows!"

The best part of these singles events may have been striking up conversations with other single women. Given that women usually outnumbered men at least three-to-one, this was not difficult. Unlike a lot of women at those events who clearly would not waste a breath or a minute diverted from the primary goal of meeting men, I happily struck up conversations with women that were as real and honest as the repartee with men tended to be shallow. Some evenings the "girl talk" urge came on sooner rather than later, having exhausted the male possibilities after the evening's first thirty minutes. We talked about our kids, child support, and jobs. "I love your shoes, where did you get them?" was always a natural entrée. (Regardless of cleavage, most women wear great shoes to these parties.) The ladies' room was also a fine place for conversation, not to mention guidance. "Watch out for the married men," a woman murmured to me, applying lipstick at the mirror one Friday night at a monthly singles event at an art museum. "You're kidding!" I answered. This was a new one to me and perked me up a bit from whatever weariness I was already experiencing after the first twenty minutes of "seeing and being seen." Hey, at least I had honesty on my side, I told myself. I really was divorced.

It never occurred to me that the one thing I *should* have feared was the embarrassment of running into my own ex-husband at one of these events, on the singles prowl himself. But there he was one Friday night at an art museum, drink in hand. I blanched, and a moment later he spotted me. As we passed each other on the pageant runway, Bill curtly nodded and lifted his glass of white wine to me, and we moved on, but not before we had exchanged small smiles at the irony of it all. I never ran into Bill at any of these again. I presume this was because after that encounter, Bill stayed away. I imagine that the only thing worse than running into one's ex-husband at a singles event might be running into one's ex-wife.

Although I found material for some good business stories and even signed up a few people for my writing workshops—including one recent widower who found a great deal of healing writing about his late wife with whom he was still deeply in love—I grew tired of these parties fairly quickly and before too long stopped going. The drinking was a little too plentiful, the conversations a little too shallow. I decided that I had better things to do with my time and my money. I eventually came to agree with one woman in the ladies room who sighed, "This is work. There's got to be a better way."

But looking back, I wouldn't give up the experience of having braved the elements, so to speak, and gone to these singles events. After every one I showed up for, I congratulated myself for simply stepping up to the plate. I learned a great deal. Not just that there were a lot of single people in the world. Not just what they did for a living. I also learned something important about myself. Each date and each singles party resulted in a triumphant revelation that I could do what I once would have thought impossible. I could do what many people dreaded and what a great many single people I knew would remain afraid to do. But for this challenge, for once, I could prove that I would not be afraid. Dating provided one more of the "Hey, I can do this!" discoveries that contributed to the secure, self-assured, and eventually loved-again person I turned out to be.

Friends with My Ex-Husband

I'll come right out and say, as a start, that my divorce was not what anyone would call amicable. Bill and I were not one of those couples who assure the world they will remain good friends before cheerily deciding to go their separate ways. Far from it. Our divorce had more than the predictable quota of bitterness and pain, fear and anger, vindictiveness and revenge. As in so many divorces where there is wealth, battles over money and property became fight-to-the-death affairs. Our lawyers were two of the most expensive in New York City, renowned for being "cutthroat" (the highest accolade anyone can give a matrimonial lawyer). An even greater expense was the gnawing anxiety, the fear-tossed nights, the tears I was not always successful in shielding from my worried, silent children. Perhaps it was not much different for my former husband.

But I don't often like to think back on those dark and

unhappy days, nor do I need to. Even though Bill plays a far less prominent role in my life today than he once did, our connection can be called—if not sometimes bordering on the unthinkably friendly—peaceable.

But here's my deep dark secret, well hidden and almost unspeakable. What I feel for him is something I could almost call . . . affection.

The truth of it is, my former husband is a good—no, he's a great father. He cares about our sons and, even more important, has put that caring into concrete, reliable action weekend after custodial weekend, band concert after orchestra concert, year after year. How could I not feel something affectionate—something even akin to love—for that one single person in the world who loves the children I would live and die for as much as I do, who would live and die for them, too?

Although I admittedly would have preferred *not* to run into him time and time again in my new life, Bill never missed a teacher conference, holiday recital, or sports event the children were involved in. He's gotten into his office late in favor of a nine o'clock in the morning "Twelve Days of Christmas" and "I Had a Little Dreidel" first grade sing-along. I sometimes smile at the thought of him, a long-time vegetarian with an aversion to meat, gingerly serving the boys their favorite chicken nuggets when they are at his house for dinner.

In my own mind, there has always been something enormously comforting about knowing that my children had someone else besides me in the world. When our youngest son had an allergic reaction requiring me to administer the dreaded EpiPen and call 9-1-1, the very

next directive to one of my other sons was "Call Dad"—
even though I knew he was in New York City and could
not meet us at the emergency room. In an uncertain
world where imagined dangers potentially befall one's
children at every moment, there is indescribable relief in
knowing that there is one other person out there in
whose care they are safe and protected, who will never let
them down, and who will never let them fall.

Sometimes today, long after the words exchanged over
issues and property have become blurred and almost forgotten, this is what I think of when I see Bill. The marriage, the good times, the bicycle and camping trips when
we were young lovers, the endless conversations and
times of laughter, the messy and awestruck births of our
children—these are long gone. I feel no affection any
longer for what we once were to each other. But what
does keep a warm flame inside me that I can't help but
recognize—much as I strive to keep it a secret—is about
what we are to each other *today*.

My ex-husband has always thought the worst of me
and probably still does. He is probably as suspicious of
my every motive today as he was throughout our nineteen-
year marriage. In a way, who can blame him? Why
wouldn't he mistrust me even today, after the role I
played in the problems that led to the end of our marriage, and after the vigorous fight for money, property,
and parental rights I put up during the divorce?

One Sunday evening some time ago, when he dropped
off our sons after a weekend that he had patiently and
arduously spent teaching Alex to ride a two-wheeler—
something I had almost given up on—I stopped him on

the way back to his car, idling in my driveway. "I just want to, need to say to you," I said, taking a breath, "I want to thank you for being the kind of father to my children—to our children—that you are."

He eyed me suspiciously. Married to this man for nineteen years, I instantly imagined his internal "What does she mean by that?"

He drew himself up with a frown and answered gruffly. "They're my children. I hardly need to be thanked."

Well, okay, some things never change. Even then, with the battles long behind us, he still mistrusted me. But for some reason I felt the need to say what needed to be said.

I answered him quietly. "All I want to say," I said slowly, touching the top of my breastbone, "is how grateful I am that my children have the kind of father that they do. For *me*," I said.

Standing there at the open door, I really didn't care if he believed it or not, or what my ulterior motive was, or any of the rest. The look on Alex's face when he had just burst through the door and announced "Mom, I can ride a two-wheeler now!" was still fresh in my mind. I simply had to express to Bill my gratitude for how devoted and diligent he had always been to work, if not alongside me, then certainly along with me, to raise the three confident, healthy, and delightful young beings that were our sons.

This time his face softened, although he looked away quickly. "Same here," he said with a nod and turned quickly back to his car.

Where Is It Written?

Not long after I was divorced, people started asking me the most astounding question. "So, are you seeing anyone new?"

The implication was that my divorced state was only a temporary glitch in the otherwise expected state of being part of a couple. Hearing this question so often made me realize that my new status as a single woman was assumed to be a highly undesirable, even unnatural state. Dangerous to the social order, perhaps, and to be remedied as quickly as possible. "Oh, you'll find someone really nice, you'll see," well-meaning relatives and acquaintances assured me.

Once I might have agreed. I had lain awake more than one night haunted by a gloomy pronouncement—it must have been a quote from some Bette Davis movie or perhaps overheard gossip between my mother and grandmother: "She never married again." Would this be my fate?

But in the months and the years after my divorce, I had slowly arrived at a startling realization. I discovered how intensely pleasurable, rewarding, and invigorating it could be to live a life without a partner to worry about pleasing. Which led me to wonder: *Why this universal assumption that I'm supposed to want to find the next man? Where is it written?*

Well, all right, so it is actually written in the Old Testament. As God ponders fashioning a companion for Adam, the lines read, "God said, 'it is not good that the man should be alone; I will make him a helper as his partner.'" But it doesn't take a Ph.D. in theology to figure out that this was clearly written by a male. Of course Adam needed a helpmate, particularly since he had quite a lot of work to do to populate the planet. But did anyone ask Eve how she felt about it? Notice God never said anything about Eve needing a partner.

I can't argue with the need to perpetuate the human species. Admittedly, this requires the collaboration of sperm and ovum. And I'll grant that when one has young offspring to raise, having a second parent around is awfully useful. Sharing expenses comes in handy, too. But for anyone either without children, or whose children have reached a certain level of independence, it can be hard to imagine why anyone would willingly give up the immensely pleasant experience of going through life strictly according to one's own dictates.

What's to love about being single and independent? Let me count the ways: Freedom to decide where and when to travel, how to spend weekends, whom to visit, or what relatives to invite over for a dinner, regardless of how boring or annoying someone else might find them. Freedom to decide how to spend my money. Coming home with a shopping bag full of some great new things from Ann Taylor that maybe I couldn't afford but that are going to make me feel dynamite, and not worrying for an instant that someone might ask or even silently wonder, *How many new clothes does she really need, anyway?* (When you're married long enough, you can always hear those thoughts.) Freedom to decide that the Queen Anne chairs look right in the family room despite someone else's insistence on a leather recliner. Complete access to the remote control. Peaceful breakfasts undisturbed by verbal updates from the morning's sports section. Driving in the car with a Norah Jones CD playing instead of the annoying rat-a-tat of a baseball announcer's radio play-by-play. Not having to worry that the leftovers I brought home from a restaurant the night before might disappear before lunch. Not bothering anyone by flossing or rattling newspapers in bed at night. Falling asleep with the papers still spread on the bed, so I can resume where I left off the next morning. Doing everything my way, every time.

But it's not all about these self-centered pleasures, either. Living independently has given me myriad opportunities to give of my time and myself, in ways that being bound to another person does not often allow. A friend calls on a Friday evening; she's just had a terrible fight with her husband, and her son is at the movies with friends. Do I want to join her for a walk, after which she'll pick up a sandwich? "Don't even think of it," I tell her. "Come on over and have dinner with me and Alex, we're sitting down in twenty minutes." After his usual fifteen-minute dinner, Alex absents himself, and my friend and I get to spend another hour or two relaxing and com-miserating. I do not give her marriage advice but simply listen. Although I had been planning an evening to myself finishing a really good book, I'm happy for the unexpected company. But even more than that, I am filled with immense satisfaction from being able to offer, to a friend I treasure having in my life, this temporary respite from what she's going through. Such moments with caring friends got me through the worst of my trou-bled marriage and divorce. They meant everything to me.

In my unmarried state, serendipitous moments like these have presented themselves again and again. Sometimes it will be a spur-of-the-minute walk with a neighbor. Or a forty-five minute catch-up call from an old college friend in California. A Saturday call to my brother who is going through his own difficult divorce and has his children for the weekend; I offer a sugges-tion: "Bring the kids over, let's go out for Chinese food." If I were sitting down to dinner with a husband, someone to whom it is understood I owe my weekend evenings, would these be possible? Hardly. Nor would my friend or brother have felt comfortable intruding on the walled-off private life of a married couple.

And then there are all those hours one aches to devote to saving the planet, feeding the hungry and homeless, curing a disease, electing a candidate, or speaking out at a town meeting—all those things that so often strain a marriage. Remember the movie *Norma Rae,* when the husband of Sally Field's character complains about being neglected because she's spending so much time organizing a union? There's Erin Brokovich, whose burning passion to earn retribution for victims of industrial pollution resulted in a barrage of complaints of emotional neglect from a boyfriend who eventually left her. "It was like watching a movie about myself," my sister Karyn told me with discomfort, recalling her round-the-clock obsession with researching and battling her son's autism. The countless exhausted hours that she put into her quest led her not only to find ways to completely reverse her son's autistic symptoms but also to write a bestselling book on autism that helped hundreds of thousands. It also strained and ultimately led to the destruction of her marriage. (A postscript: From an online, global network of other autism parents with whom Karyn became connected as the result of her work, she fell in love over the Internet with the father of an autistic child in another country. Besides being someone who shared her passion, this man was, in Karyn's words, her soul mate. She relocated and they married and now remain about the most in-love married couple I know.)

And what about love? Am I advocating for independence over love? Not exactly. Love is a grand and wonderful thing. But I'll say this. When you fall in love and get married, there's gain but there's also loss. Like everything else in life, wedding oneself to a partner comes with a cost.

Admittedly, there is one pitfall of remaining unmarried. The pleasures of being single can be awfully hard to give up.

Opening My Heart

It did seem curious, even to me, that so many years had passed since my divorce without my entering any kind of romantic relationship with a man. The simple truth was I didn't miss it. I knew that the next relationship was something I *should* want, so I went through the motions. When friends offered to fix me up with single men, I accepted. It had been years since I had bothered with online dating, which I eventually gave up entirely, glad for all the hours that had been freed up from writing pointless, time-wasting e-mails to strangers. When I had a particularly empty weekend or the spirit moved me, I still occasionally ventured out to an adult singles party. Though many men appeared presentable enough, not once did my heart go aflutter at the sight of an attractive man. Once in a while someone would ask for my phone number but nothing ever went beyond one or two dates. Although I dated many perfectly acceptable men, I never developed the slightest romantic or physical attraction to any of them—not so much as a crush.

When I did go out on a date, I probably ended up frustrating a good many men who were interested in an evening that might turn romantic. What usually happened instead was that not long into the date—usually over before-dinner drinks—my date and I would exchange information about what each of us did for a living. Within minutes, my business reporter's curiosity would kick in and I would find myself interviewing my date about every aspect of his job or business. What had interested him about going into oncology instead of something more upbeat? How had the family tobacco business gotten started? And how interesting to learn that tobacco had once been widely grown in Connecticut, whereas I had always assumed tobacco was grown only in the deep South. How were marine hardware sales doing in this economy, given the recession in the shipping industry? Once, while dancing with the editor of a financial newsletter at a meet-and-mingle singles dance on the Upper East Side of Manhattan—to the throbbing backdrop of Marvin Gaye's "I Heard It Through the Grapevine"—I received my dance partner's perspective on why the labor shortage was exerting no upward pressure on wage levels. (I was to use this as a sidebar in my next week's article in a local business journal. I even called him on Monday for a follow-up, on-the-record quote, in a brief conversation in which the topic of a date never came up.) Even when I didn't have a particular writing project in mind, I relished learning about the various jobs men held and companies I had never known a thing about. Needless to say these conversations were completely devoid of sexual promise. Not surprisingly, I was rarely asked out on a second date.

I recognized that I seemed to be spinning my wheels. I was single; I was supposed to be looking for a new relationship, right? But over time, the problem became clear. I had been going after something I really didn't want.

The simple explanation was that I was enjoying my unattached state immensely. The dark days of the divorce were behind me, and my life felt very full and, for the first time in years, peaceful. It still seemed a daily miracle to wake up each day to fresh air instead of the dank smell of a dying relationship. There was no one in my life to criticize or berate me; my days were filled only with my delightfully growing sons and my friends—all people who loved and appreciated me, and let me know it.

Because the boys were with Bill part of every week and on alternate weekends, I appreciated my sons all the more when I had them. Although I had braced myself for the worst when they entered adolescence, they were instead turning into delightful, funny, and interesting teenagers. I loved being able to give them all my time and attention when we were all together and could hardly imagine introducing a strange man onto the scene. On weekends when I didn't have the boys with me, my time off from work and parenting was spent happily alone, either catching up on a writing assignment, reading, writing, walking at the beach, or doing errands. If the house ever got too quiet, I had a multitude of friends, both single and married, to call for a walk, a movie, or one of the free outdoor concerts that my town offers every summer. I happily discovered perhaps the Number One benefit of divorce—just ask any divorced parent: when the children are with the other custodial parent, you can go anywhere without the guilt or expense of hiring a babysitter. Although I sometimes rented videos, often to catch up on "chick flick" movies that I would rarely drag a date to, they were usually returned unwatched. Life had gotten too interesting to spend time watching TV.

From time to time I even found myself wondering what possible reason there was for wanting to have a man in my life, anyway. Who needed the headache? I could barely remember what it was that made people want to be in love. Every so often, there would be a moment I would be stirred, such as whenever I listened to my CD of Jussi Björling and Robert Merrill singing the duet from *The Pearl Fishers*. The sweet, rich maleness of their voices, one tenor, one baritone, would remind me of something from long ago. *Yes,* I would think, *I could love a man again.* Although there was no one in my life at that moment, it was reassuring to know that there was still inside me, like a pilot light, a tiny flame burning very low.

But after rebuilding this rich, new life after my divorce, I felt that little, if anything, was missing. I occasionally worried that I was becoming too independent. How would I ever be able to give up this delightful freedom to live according to my own schedule? Would I even be able to cater to a man's needs or listen to his problems?

I can tell you the exact day I decided that I was ready to welcome love back into my life. It was September 11, 2001.

It was a bright, gorgeous Tuesday morning, two days after my birthday.

As usual, David and Robert had left early for high school, and I had just returned to an empty house after putting Alex on the elementary school bus. I ran upstairs to turn off the TV left on in my bedroom. But there was something terribly odd and wrong. On the small screen, the World Trade Center was spewing smoke and flames from a huge hole ripped through one of the towers. White specks of debris like confetti were also showering from the building, just below the line of flames. The picture was eerily silent, which struck me as odd, given the violence of the smoke and the flames shooting from the building. Because there was no sound, the flames had almost a peaceful licking motion, like a winter fireplace. I froze, then brought my hand to my mouth. My heart began to pound, almost entirely filling my chest. A thought came to me that was completely unreal and, at the same time, profoundly sickening. *There are people in there. What about all those people in there?*

Years before, I had worked on the thirty-fourth floor of the Deutsche Bank building—then it was called Bankers Trust building—across a narrow street from the south tower of the World Trade Center. Many times a day, glancing up from my desk, I would look directly into what were actually very ordinary offices in its gleaming south tower. It was almost comical, really, how close we seemed, given how high above the ground each of our offices were. Across the chasm between us, I could practically see every wastebasket, computer terminal, and white board. And people—many ordinary office workers just like those alongside me. Through the slatted World Trade Center windows I could see messengers wheeling carts. Young men leaning on desks. Women and men standing in coffee lines and then bringing the cups back to their cubicles. Secretaries answering phones. It was almost like looking in a mirror, those offices were so similar to mine.

The flames continued to lick the huge hole in the side of the tower. The newscasters' voices were low and controlled, but there were often long silences when they had little to say.

I reached for the phone. I had to call someone—but whom? This wasn't a bit of news you just passed on to a friend or neighbor. I wanted to talk to someone close to me, someone intimate—the one person you would not be embarrassed to grab in a scary movie or when the airplane hit turbulence. My sister—yes, I could call Karyn. Before I could reach for the phone, hands shaking, there was a quick, dark flash on the screen, and then a huge ball of black smoke. Before my eyes, the second tower was hit.

I began to tremble and sank to the side of my bed. What was happening? This couldn't be.

Suddenly the reporter from the Pentagon came onto the screen. "I don't want to scare anybody, but there's just been an explosion here," he said. His voice had an urgency I had never heard before.

I could not bear to be alone another minute.

Heart still pounding, I left my house and ran across the street to my friend Shirlee's house. Shirlee was also alone; her son Josh was at high school along with my sons.

Shirlee's face at the door was white. "I've been speaking to Howard," she said of her husband who works in lower Manhattan. "He's been standing out on the street and watching people jumping from windows. He's very shook up. They were jumping, right in front of him." She had no idea whether Howard would be coming home or whether anyone would be able to get home. Public transportation had been halted.

I asked Shirlee if she would come across the street to my house so that neither of us would be alone. She picked up her house key, then stopped short. "No, no . . . I need to stay here by the phone in case Josh calls from school," she said. She was right. What if they were sending the children home from school? I had to get home.

I headed back across the street. Under a crisp, blue sky, the street was dappled with shade from maple and cottonwood trees, thick with late summer foliage. The day was as warm and gorgeous as I had ever seen a September day.

The phone was ringing—it was my friend Linda, about a mile away. "Ken's at a meeting. I'm alone here. Can I bring my lunch over?"

"Of course," I said. Lunch.

I was always grateful for the excuse to leave the Bankers Trust building at lunchtime; my job bored me. Every day, I would cross the street to eat at one of the food courts in the World Trade Center's lower level. The bustle and energy of those wide passageways streaming with people on lunch break, the flashes of color and sounds, and the smells of food were a relief from the tedium of my job at the bank. It was like a subterranean city unto itself, with its own post office and zip code.

Those corridors and the shimmering white marble lobby above became my own small, busy town where I took care of many ordinary tasks. Mario shined my shoes and replaced my heels in a shoe repair shop whose dark, crowded interior looked far too ancient to be located in a modern office building. To delay going back to my office, I would cruise a luggage store, meander through Rite Aid, buy a card or two at the Hallmark store.

In the morning and then again after five o'clock, I would cross the lobby heading to the Seventh Avenue IRT line World Trade Center subway stop. That small corner of lower Manhattan became as familiar to me as the Upper West Side streets of Manhattan where I grew up.

Back in my bedroom, I watched one tower fall in a thick cloud of gray dust and then another. My city was being destroyed.

Having the boys come home from school later that afternoon offered curiously little comfort. David and Robert were mostly annoyed that their high school principal had not allowed any of the students to know what was going on—a precaution, it turned out, due to the fact that several students' parents worked in the World Trade Center.

"Remember our day at the World Trade Center, Rob?" I asked my thirteen-year-old son.

When Robert was eight, it was his turn to spend a day alone with me in New York City, for lunch and a Broadway show. It was something I did once a year with each of the children when they were young enough to miss an occasional day of school. The show Robert picked was *Cats;* I was dubious, but he had assured me, quoting the TV commercial verbatim, that *Cats* was the most exciting theatrical event ever to reach Broadway. I had bought great seats in the first row of the mezzanine. Five minutes into the show, an actor with glowing eyes dressed in a cat costume pounced onto the balcony railing two feet away from us. Robert jumped and began to cry. After one boring song after another, the first act finally ended. Robert turned to me. "Can we leave?" he whispered. "Yes!" I replied instantly.

But how to salvage our special day together? "Let's go downtown, to the top of the World Trader Center," I said. Robert readily agreed; he had never been there. A quick subway ride later, we were there. It was the perfect day for it, with only a short line of people in the white marble lobby for the shuddering elevator that sped to the 110th floor. The sky was clear and we marveled at being able see miles and miles in each direction, over wide bodies of water, the Statue of Liberty, the skyscrapers of Manhattan and Central Park. We stayed for an hour or more, first on one side of the building, then another. Robert was amazed at the thickness of the white television antenna up close; from the ground, it looked like a needle. We had our photo taken together against a fake Manhattan backdrop and brought home souvenirs. We always thought of the World Trade Center as our special place.

Now five years later, Robert kept his face impassive when I told him, still not believing it myself, that there was no World Trade Center any more.

Shortly afterward, Bill's car was in the driveway to pick them up. It was Tuesday, the day the boys always went to Bill's house to sleep over. Columbine had happened on a Tuesday, too. I remembered having been terribly shook up all that afternoon, since the teenagers who were slaughtered that day in their high school library were the same ages as my high school sons. I had found it difficult to be alone in my house. But that night was nothing like the one to come.

My empty house was a terrible place to be that night of September 11. Never did I feel so bereft and adrift, so sickeningly unprotected and frightened, as I did sitting awake in my dark bedroom most of the night transfixed, eyes on the TV. My arms were clutched around me tightly, as though to keep everything inside me from spilling out. The hours dragged on, as the mayor and police chief held shell-shocked news conferences. Estimates of the rising body count crawled across the bottom of the screen. The pressure of my own arms around me was all the comfort I could give myself. It wasn't much. I could not make sense of my thoughts. But I did know that I was desperate for one thing above all else. I wanted to be held by strong arms. I wanted not to be let go.

I had known loneliness in my life. But never an aloneness like I felt that night. It was like an actual, bleeding wound. I felt overwhelmed with a sense of vulnerability that was at once unfamiliar and piercing. In my mind, over and over, I replayed the scene of those buildings collapsing in a cloud of gray-black dust. First one, then the other. The impossible had happened. Which meant that anything could happen.

Over the next few days, I was filled with an underlying sense of fear that no amount of being with my children or friends could assuage. We all felt that way, I knew that.

It helped to gather with friends and to share our thoughts. Living only an hour from New York City, to which many people in my town commuted, I heard reports of many friends and acquaintances who had lost people in the World Trade Center. A friend lost her brother, a father of four. The wife of a good friend arrived late to work that day, needing to hem a pair of pants; when she arrived, the building was on fire and 315 people in her company had perished. Two women in my town were now widows. The father of my son's friends was a stockbroker who worked on Wall Street and was having a hard time of it; he had, in his wife's words "lost all his buds." I felt immensely grateful to have lost no one close to me. My brother Matthew worked in midtown Manhattan and had been able to get through to us to let us know he was all right before making what was to be a twelve-hour trip back to his home in Brooklyn.

Several days later, I took the train into New York City. In Grand Central Station, tacked up on a long wall that had been temporarily constructed with folded screens in the middle of a passageway, were hundreds of photocopied Missing Persons flyers with grainy photos of lost loved ones. I stopped, arrested, and began to read them. For a long time, I went from one to the other. A younger brother who just became a rookie fireman. A son, in his first job. A mother and grandmother. A father of three. A daughter, just graduated from high school. And wives and husbands—especially many husbands.

It took almost an hour to be able to walk away from those photos of all those lost husbands and wives.

On the train home, I thought long and hard about my

life these last seven years. How good it had been to be free of a bad marriage, and to be living a life of my own creation, of only pleasantness and peace. How thrilling it had been to discover so many strengths and abilities I might never have known that I had. The discovery that I could forge my own happiness, that I didn't need a lover or a husband to be happy, had been liberating and, even at times, intoxicating.

But now something had changed. Once I had thought—we had all thought—that our country was powerful, invulnerable. With wide oceans protecting us on either side, along with our superior form of government and an invincible military, we were utterly safe from harm. Nothing bad could ever happen to us here, I believed. Hadn't we all believed that?

But the impossible had happened. Our vulnerability had been ripped open and exposed to the world. Like those towers, I, too, felt as though I had been ripped open, and there was now a place, gaping and open to the world, that ached to be filled. I needed to find comfort and to connect in the deepest possible way.

But to invite a man into my life again—to enter into a state of deep intimacy—could I risk another failed relationship? Until now, perhaps not. But that reluctance paled in comparison to the greater fear about what might yet happen in what had suddenly become a dangerous and unstable world. It was more than just needing strong arms around me. I wanted someone in my corner, to face alongside me whatever was yet to befall us.

I ached to find that person.

Over the next few days, a poem I had not thought of in

years, Matthew Arnold's "Dover Beach," entered my mind repeatedly. "Ah, love, let us be true/ To one another! for the world, which seems/ To lie before us like a land of dreams/ So various, so beautiful, so new/ Hath really neither joy, nor love, nor light,/ Nor certitude, nor peace, nor help for pain . . . "

Then I knew. Putting up with someone else's needs or problems—risking love with all its pitfalls and perils—would be a small price to pay for the arms around me I needed, but had not had, on that terrible September night.

I was ready for love. It was time to open my heart.

Then Comes Love

And then one day it all becomes worth it—all the fears and the struggle, the loneliness and yearning, the fighting and the escape and all that comes in between. It all becomes valuable and meaningful because it brings you to this place—this crest at the top of the long, exhausting hill, this new beginning, this exhilarating glimpse of the pleasure-filled life that can come again. Then comes love—the prize at the end, the reward for getting through it all. It is the place of rest, the place of bliss, the place where the miracle occurs.

I met Bob when I was ready for love and not a moment before. Several years had gone by in which I had hoped and sometimes even yearned for it. I thought I was ready and that I had opened my heart for it. Many times I was impatient. But once again, God or the universe or whatever it was that had guided and protected me so far had a different timetable.

For a short time, I had been in a relationship with a

kind and interesting man who made it very clear from
the outset that he had no interest in marriage. I told him,
quite truthfully, that that was perfectly fine with me.
Although I was more than ready for a loving relationship, I wasn't ready to think about marriage either. To
give up my independence, to permanently share my
home, particularly my delightfully empty double bed in
which I woke up every morning alongside the newspapers I had fallen asleep reading the night before? Uh . . .
perhaps not. This mutual understanding didn't stop us
from enjoying each other's company. Spending weekends together, along with the occasional weeknight when
I didn't have my kids and he didn't have a meeting, was
a major enhancement to my life. He was the most intelligent and interesting man I knew, and our shared interest in a great many things, everything from politics to
radio shows featuring music of the 1930s and 1940s,
filled our time together with many lively discussions and
much easygoing fun.

But in the time that we dated, while living apart and
maintaining very separate lives, something in me began
to change. For the first time in many years, I began to
remember some of those things that make people want
to share life with a partner. Sunday mornings, reading
the newspapers without having to talk, with classical
music in the background. Having a man to cook for and
to do small, thoughtful errands for. I would walk past
Brooks Brothers and glance wistfully inside to the tables
neatly stacked with neckties. It had been years since I had
picked out a man's tie.

One morning, while in New Orleans for a three-day

public relations conference, I was walking down a quiet street from my hotel to the convention center. A small, neon sign jutted from the building with the name of a restaurant—*Mother's*—that I recognized as a tourist destination well-known for its Louisiana breakfasts. As I passed the restaurant, the door opened. Along with the aromas of dark-roasted coffee and honey cured ham, the sounds of a sizzling griddle and clattering silverware spilled out onto the street. And there were voices—conversations shouted on top of conversations in a cascade of voices chattering, laughing, and competing to be heard above the din. Maybe it was the name of the restaurant that made me think about my children and wonder what they were doing this Sunday morning at their father's house. Or perhaps it was all the laughter and shouting that caused a single word to come to me: *family*. These were families. Having breakfast together, as families do.

I thought of my own at home. The family I had been part of, which since the divorce consisted only of me and my three sons, seemed to be dissolving as quickly as lather held under water between my fingers. First David had left for college, and then in the blink of an eye, it seemed, Robert had gone as well. With only Alex now remaining at home, I was often struck by how different my home had become from the busy, boisterous place it had once been. The handwriting was on the wall. In just a few more years, Alex would be gone, too.

What was I doing here, standing alone outside a restaurant on a New Orleans street? I wanted to be part of a family again.

It was one thing to come to the conclusion, that day,

that I did want to be married again. But it was another thing entirely to make peace with it. Everything about my past marriage and divorce cautioned me against it. Why risk all that pain again? Why give up my independence and this terrific life I had made for myself? But I could no longer keep from myself the guilty secret that I *did* want to find serious love again. This presented a dilemma. How could I reconcile this desire for love—all right, this somewhat embarrassing need for love—with my unwillingness to ever put myself in the position of needing anyone or anything again? I wrestled with the problem but, after returning from New Orleans, said nothing to the man I was dating. Instead, for no reason, I found myself beginning to find fault with things he did or didn't do.

One day in late summer, I returned home from a week away to find all the petunias in front of my house shriveled and dead. For some illogical reason, this had me feeling baffled and slightly outraged. All my hard work planting those gorgeous purple and white petunias! And now they were dead. I felt betrayed, almost. It only took a few moments for logic to intercede. What did I expect? It had been a hot, dry week, and the petunias had not been watered.

Then it hit me. The petunias didn't apologize for needing water. The petunias weren't embarrassed that they needed water. If I decided that my petunias, through the force of my own resolve and willpower, would never need anyone or anything again, that would do absolutely nothing to keep them from ending up dead. Petunias needed water to live. It was that simple.

I gradually came to understand and accept that my desire for love, like my petunias' need for water, was a fact of life. Not a sign of weakness, but a basic human impulse. Part of nature's plan.

And what about repeating past mistakes? What about the risk of loving someone and possibly losing him? There was risk in this, too, I knew. I remembered all those flyers in Grand Central Station with the smiling faces of dead fiancés, husbands, wives. The greater the love, the greater the risk of loss, my wise philosopher-therapist once told me. He had posed a question. If we were truly to avoid this risk, would anyone ever have children?

I had been through so much with the divorce. Could I face that kind of loss as well?

This would take courage. But with all these years behind me, the financial negotiations, moving and establishing myself in a new town, building a new career, raising my children on my own, traveling alone, traipsing out to singles dances, all those blind dates—with all that behind me, courage was something I knew I had.

With much regret, because I came to understand that my current relationship would never lead to the new family that I wanted to create, I eventually let go of it.

Some time afterward, I went to a business networking breakfast in a nearby city. Aside from a few familiar faces with whom I was able to catch up, most of the attendees were strangers. After coffee, bagels, and informal chatting and exchange of business cards ("Hi, I'm Jessica Bram, tell me about your business . . . "), the group's organizer, an attorney, called the meeting to order. He

instructed us to stand one at a time and introduce ourselves to the group. "After telling us a little bit about your
business, please tell the group the one thing that you feel
would be helpful to get from this meeting," he said.

As luck would have it, I happened to be seated at the
end of a row and was therefore the first called upon to
introduce myself. I didn't have even a moment to think
about how to answer that question. What would I like to
get from this meeting? I blurted out the first thing that
came to mind. "Well, I was just telling my friend Wilder
here that I recently ended a relationship. I'd like to start
dating someone new. So if anyone knows anyone . . . "

An embarrassed silence and then laughter all around.
Oh, God, I thought, *where did that come from?* That was
completely inappropriate. This is a business meeting. I
shut my eyes and, with a wan smile, sank to my chair. I
was too distracted by my own embarrassment to hear
another single introduction. And then I relaxed. *Oh, what
the hell,* I thought. *We're all human.* Finally the last person
in the circle, an attractive young blonde woman, stood
for her turn. "I'd like to date someone, too," she said.
Suddenly this business meeting had a much friendlier
tone than the usual networking get-together. Even the
speaker seemed more relaxed than usual when he got up
to address the group.

Later that afternoon, I received a phone call from the attorney who led the group. "Jessica, I don't know you at all, but
you seem like a reasonable person. I was thinking I might
give your number to a friend of mine named Brian who's
recently been divorced. I've also got a single brother who
lives in Boston. But first let me tell you about Brian . . . "

By that point I had received at least three similar assurances from friends or business acquaintance that with my permission, they would like to give my phone number to some single or recently divorced friend, brother, or associate. I had yet to receive a single call. "Of course, go right ahead," I told the attorney, exactly as I had said to the others. Then I forgot all about it.

Though newly separated, Brian never did call, having begun dating someone just about the same time as my networking breakfast (thus once again demonstrating the lightning-quick shelf life of the unattached male). But several months later, I received an e-mail from the attorney's brother in Boston. It took a few moments to remember the connection. Then the networking breakfast came back to me. Maybe I hadn't been such an idiot after all.

Bob and I met for dinner at a restaurant halfway between my house and his brother's, where he was in town visiting for the weekend. He told me to expect someone who looked not at all like his brother, which was not difficult since I had by then completely forgotten what his brother looked like. When I walked up to the bar, however, Bob recognized me immediately from the photo on my website—which I will admit to having chosen carefully for just such an eventuality. (Having one's own business website was so much more subtle, I had decided, than posting one's photo on an online dating site.) We started talking, and the conversation continued—through dinner and coffee, then later at a nearby live music café. When the music became unbearably awful and too loud to talk over, we walked down the block to a quieter restaurant, where we sat at the bar and talked some more.

He had been divorced five years and had two sons, teenage boys close in age to mine. This in itself was an immediate attraction—I was nothing less than in love with my three teenage sons and relished the idea of getting to know two more. Best of all, Bob had a serious musical life along with his day job. He was a pianist and keyboard player who played professionally on weekends at everything from large rock and doo-wop shows at concert halls, to bars and weddings. I told him I would love to hear him play. He told me he wanted to read my writing.

I got home just after midnight, feeling slightly dazed. An out-of-town friend, Joni, who was staying with me for the weekend, had waited up for me. "I had a really nice time," I said, as though there was something puzzling and slightly miraculous about this. Where had the hours gone? And how unusual to arrive home from a blind date without the usual muttered "Thank God that's over," as I kicked off my shoes and poured myself my normal bedtime cup of herbal tea.

"Nice guy," I told Joni. "I liked him." Then I floated upstairs, still wearing my shoes and completely forgetting about tea.

Bob called the next morning from his car on his way back to Boston. Despite all the talking we had done the night before, we were both a little tongue-tied on the phone. I tried to conjure up his face but better remembered his tall build and broad shoulders as we had walked alongside each other back to our cars parked alongside each other in the restaurant lot. He was much taller than me. I liked that.

After the "I had a good time last night" formalities, we

ran out of things to say. There was a pause over the telephone. Then, once again, I found myself blurting out words I hadn't planned. "What are you doing driving back to Boston? You're going in the wrong direction," I said.

His answer was immediate. "Want me to turn around?"

Reason got the better of me. "No, no, of course not. I have plans today . . . my son comes back . . . you've got to get home." I was back to normal.

The next few weeks went by in a dazed blur—another quick visit the following Sunday, where we met in a town halfway between Boston and my Connecticut town, over an hour's drive for each. There were phone calls, lots of e-mails, and more phone calls. We wouldn't see each other for another three weeks, at least; he would be leaving soon for a weeklong cruise to Bermuda, where he would be part of the entertainment crew. By the time he left for the cruise, we were speaking and e-mailing several times a day. He spent a fortune on ship-to-shore phone calls and expensive Internet connections, e-mailing me from the cruise ship.

I sent him a few of my essays. He told me later that when he read them, he knew his fate was sealed. When I finally got to hear him play at a resort in Maine about a month later, I was practically knocked breathless by his talent and musicality, and I realized mine was sealed as well. Away from the music, when we were alone together, I remembered for the first time in—how long? I could not even remember—what it was that made people search for, and never give up hope for, love.

Kitchens II

W hen I was a child I used to look at the old people sitting on park benches on the islands on Broadway, or the middle-aged people on the crosstown bus, and I used to think, *How do they stand it? How can they bear being old, knowing that so much of their lives are behind them, with no hope of romance, no great unwritten future?*

I smile at this as I sit at my table today in my kitchen flooded with sunlight. Last year, with some money I was able to put aside from my business and a small inheritance from my father, I decided to renovate my tiny kitchen. The cheap Formica cabinets have been replaced by glass-front cabinets that display my grandmother's casserole dish and the tag sale oddities I have collected over the years. I splurged on a better quality oven from which I turn out wonderful dishes that still never seem to finish cooking all at the same time. There is now a center island with two high stools where my sons can perch to watch a ball game on the small TV or where friends sip wine while I cook.

But best of all, once the kitchen was enlarged, I was able to make room for the old butcher block table that had been kept in storage since the divorce. The reassembled table has been newly sanded and oiled. Although it does not look new, the oak glows warm and golden. The table brings back all the memories of my boys' early childhood years—moving to table from highchairs, then to booster seats, then finally to "big boy" chairs. It is the table where we laughed and lit Shabbat candles and shared challah and strawberries and the occasional splurge of a chocolate mousse cake. There is no sadness in the memory that this is the table, too, where Bill once sat at the head. He has a table of his own now, in another house not far away. Every other Friday night, he and our sons light Shabbat candles there, too.

Today, my older boys come together at this table when they are home from college. Our dinner table is much like it was when they were younger, when the boys would make each other laugh silly over some private joke the three of them understood that totally excluded me but got me laughing nonetheless just at the sheer pleasure of watching them. And this is the table where my new love, the man I will marry next year, lifts his glass, one arm around me, on Friday nights, as we sing the blessing over the wine together.

Today, this kitchen and this house, where my sons and I made a new home after what I now think of as not the end but the rebirth of our family, are continually filled with friends and family and joyful times. Sun streams through the windows and bathes the oak table top; and I say to myself, *Yes, I can stand it. I can certainly bear this being older, with all those hard times behind me, all that sadness and all that struggle. Here at this moment, in this sunlit kitchen, in this safe spot, I am blessed.* This is what I wish I could have told that tear-stained woman who once faced the loss of a family, a dream home, and a dream kitchen. I wish I could have told her that this day would surely come when I—when all of us—are truly, finally, home.

Epilogue: A New Lexicon

Ever since my marriage ended more than a decade ago, I have been continually struck by the dreadful reaction that the word *divorced* seems to elicit. "I'm *so* sorry," I was told, again and again—not only when I first announced the fact of my former husband's and my decision but in all the ensuing years since. The response was as though somebody had died. Or like the sympathetic neighbor's dismal proclamation "And we thought you were such a nice family!" the message was that we had revealed ourselves as fundamentally flawed.

Yes, divorce was hard. The long into-the-night discussions with my former spouse, separating our belongings and our bank accounts, facing the dismal financial compromises that come with splitting one household into two—it surely was one of the most difficult times I've ever gone through. Worse, of course, was knowing that we were putting our children through the wrench of having their homes and lives disrupted. There was no getting around the fact that for our three young sons, our divorce was a sad turn of events.

I'm not minimizing the pain and challenges of divorce. But divorce is not death. Far from it.

My divorce was a transformation and a blessing in so many ways. After many years of trying unsuccessfully to make a relationship what it was not, it was a profound relief to finally let go. And then came the exhilarating challenge of building a new life for myself and our children. Getting divorced meant finally being able to choose where and how I wanted to live, and where I wanted my sons to grow up. Being on my own, both physically and financially, was at times terrifying, yes. But it also offered exhilarating opportunities to test my limits and grow. And my sons, facing real hurdles for the first time in their young lives, grew and strengthened as well.

It also gave my former husband the opportunity to finally find someone who loved him the way he deserved to be loved. What a great pity it would be for him to have gone through his life without that.

I tell my friends, who feel trapped in bad marriages but terrified of divorce, to fear not. Divorce means a second chance, or maybe even a third or fourth chance, at happiness. Divorce is not the problem but a solution, when all else fails, to irreparable marital unhappiness. Facing a divorce, calling a spade a spade, minimizing one's losses, cashing in the chips when the alternative is to lose it all—whatever one wants to call it—is one of the most adult, responsible actions a person can take in life. Facing up to divorce means no longer allowing oneself to regret the past or whine about the present. Divorce means taking that first constructive action, no matter how hard, expensive, or demoralizing that can be, toward building a new future. Not just for oneself, but for one's children as well. Because children deserve to live in a home of peace, loving feelings, and tranquility.

Now more than a decade after our marriage ended, my former husband and I are no longer mismatched, battling spouses, but peaceable colleagues. Most of all, we are cooperative co-parents, with the single, unified purpose of making the best lives possible for our treasured sons. This, I believe, is what we are at our best, and what we were meant to be.

Perhaps it's time to simply retire that miserable word itself, *divorce*. The word is an antique, something like the word *wedlock*, which suggests shackles into which husband and wife are permanently locked. Think about it: Of all of life's major events—birth, marriage, death—only one event, divorce, connotes two things at once. Divorce is both a death *and* a birth, a loss *and* a gain, an ending *and* a beginning. Divorce is, in fact, a turnaround in life. Like the Greek god Janus, from which January is derived, divorce has two faces—one looking backward, one forward.

Divorce is also a precipice—a balancing spot—unsteady though it may feel at times—from which to leap forward into a better future. So why use a word to describe it that only signals the backward part, the wrenching apart, the one that contains the loss?

Let's come up with a better word to describe that stage of life that is not death at all but a turning point. A more cheerful word that signals not only the ending of what came before, but that possibility-filled time that comes after. We're good at coming up with euphemisms, after all. A person who has lost a job is "in transition." People are no longer "handicapped," but "physically challenged."

What do we say instead? "Reborn"? "Recharged?" "Reoriented?" "Re-singled?"

Call me anything, but please don't call me "divorced." And *don't* call me unhappy.

About the Author

Jessica Bram is a writer, radio commentator, and essayist whose work has been published and syndicated in national and regional newspapers and magazines, including *The New York Times*, *NY Times* HERS column, *Child Magazine*, *Country Accents*, and the Gannett Newspapers. Her radio commentaries—which have twice earned her first prize in the radio commentary category of the Connecticut Society of Professional Journalists' "Excellence in Journalism" competition—are frequently heard on the National Public Radio station WSHU during NPR's *All Things Considered* and *Morning Edition*.

Jessica has been a freelance journalist and editor, and former special sections editor of the *Fairfield County (Conn.) Business Journal*. As founder of Jessica Bram Communications, she provided public relations services to businesses and served as communications director of local political campaigns. She began her career as a New York City Urban Fellow assigned to the Office of the Mayor.

Besides giving hope and encouragement to people either facing or fearing divorce, Jessica's personal mission is to empower other writers to find and use their creative voices. As founder of the Westport Writers'

Workshop, she teaches workshops in creative nonfiction, memoir, and essay writing. Information about these and other workshops, including fiction and magazine writing, can be found on www.westportwritersworkshop.com.

Jessica received both bachelor of arts and masters' degrees from Cornell University. She lives in Connecticut with her three sons, all of whom regularly provide her with personal essay material.

Jessica invites readers to contribute and subscribe to her *Happily Ever After* blog, which contain reflections, resources, and inspiring thoughts about creating a great life after divorce. The blog can be found on www.jbram.com/blog or at www.happilyeverafterdivorce.com.